Just Clowning Around

Sharing God's Love Through Laughter

Janice P. Petrea

Woman's Missionary Union
Birmingham, Alabama

Woman's Missionary Union
P. O. Box 830010
Birmingham, AL 35283-0010

Woman's Missionary Union®, WMU®, and Acteens® are registered trademarks.

Dewey Decimal Classification: 259.23
SUBJECT HEADINGS: CHURCH WORK WITH YOUTH
                  WITNESSING
                  MINISTRY
                  CLOWNS
                  SKITS

Unless otherwise noted, all Scripture quotations are from the Holy Bible, New International Version (NIV). Copyright ©1973, 1978, 1984 International Bible Society. Used by permission of Zondervan Bible Publishers.

Cover design by Janell E. Young
Photography by Picture Perfect (Don Cole), Advance, NC
Illustrations in chapter 5 and illustrations on handouts 7 and 8 by Ronnie Pinyan

ISBN: 1-56309-237-9
W986101•0498•5M1

TO THE GLORY OF GOD

and

in gratitude to Misty McNeill and the Acteens' "Clowns 4 Christ" (1992–93) at First Baptist Church in Troy, North Carolina, for sharing insights, talents, and the encouragement that inspired the birth of a new clowning ministry at my church and ultimately this book

and

in love to all the members of the Faith Baptist Church Clowning Ministry and especially to Stacy Brawley, Sarah Chandler, Ann Eagle, Jenny Flowe, Kelly Hunsucker, Elizabeth Jones, Joy Little, April Moody Chandler, Ginny Petrea, and Bryan Snyder for serving faithfully with me on my first Acteens Activators missions experience and for allowing me to see the love of Jesus firsthand through their ministry of clowning

and

in admiration and love to Becky Brawley, my constant clowning companion, "ringmaster extraordinaire," faithful prayer warrior, and most treasured friend.

CONTENTS

Introduction 1

Chapter 1: Clowning as a Witnessing Tool for Youth 3

Chapter 2: What Is Christian Clowning? 5

Chapter 3: Organizing a Clowning Ministry for Youth 7

Chapter 4: Clowning Basics 14

Chapter 5: Makeup and Costumes 24

Chapter 6: Planning for Props, Skits, and Programs 31

Chapter 7: Ministry Ideas 36

Appendix A: Sample Skits 39

Appendix B: An Initial Clowning Workshop for Youth 69

Resources and Bibliography 92

INTRODUCTION

"There is . . . a time to weep and a time to laugh" (Eccl. 3: 1,4 NIV).

It had been a long week of missions work for the youth team at Carolina Beach, North Carolina. With their last clowning program at the amusement park completed, the overpowering desire for something cold and sweet to eat that had been building throughout the evening was now too much to bear. As the last of the props and equipment were loaded into the church van, the small troupe of young clowns, adorned in complete makeup and costume, agreed to go for ice cream . . . just for fun.

Judging from the long line that greeted them at the ice-cream shop, their idea had apparently been shared by many that night. As the clowns waited in the entryway, children nearby began to giggle and wave. Naturally, there was nothing to do but return the silly antics. From one side, a woman's voice was heard. "Oh, look. Clowns. Maybe they can make Tina laugh."

The woman and her husband had entered the shop with two small girls—one with a smiling face, bouncing auburn curls, and a timid wave for the unexpected clowns. The other had the same bouncing auburn curls but no timid wave, not even a faint smile. In fact, she hid her face in her mother's skirt as the family waited for a vacant table.

As space became available, the youth clowns found themselves seated in close view of the two girls and their parents. One of the clowns noticed two dark, peering eyes staring at her just over the edge of the booth seat. She responded to the stare by playing a game of peekaboo from behind her menu, causing the little girl to giggle and squirm in her seat. Another clown remembered the prizes remaining from the amusement park and went to the church van to retrieve them. It was a spur of the moment thought.

With prizes in hand, the clowns left their table and approached the family, giving each girl a smile, a small sticker, and a friendship bracelet with the words Jesus Loves You. *After a few minutes of conversation, the waitress arrived with the family's ice-cream order and the clowns returned to their own table. They watched as the shyest of the girls turned timidly toward them, smiled ever so slightly, and wiggled her small fingers in a bashful wave.*

It was hard to understand the tears filling that mother's eyes or why her smile was one of melancholy happiness instead of joyful laughter. Later, as her family prepared to leave, the woman approached the clowns.

"I just had to come over and thank you. You don't know what you've done for Tina—for all of us tonight. You see, Tina and her sister are our foster children. They came to us from a situation of sexual abuse, and Tina has become severely withdrawn. She hasn't laughed in months, and for weeks now we haven't even seen her smile. We have been so

worried about her. Tonight, you gave her joy. That's something Tina hasn't had for a long, long time. I know God is with you. Thank you. Thank you for Tina's smile."

A clowning ministry is much more than a program of skits; more than animal balloons or magic tricks; more than greasepaint and baggy pants. Hearts committed to serving God take advantage of even the most unexpected opportunities and use them for His glory. The situation at the ice-cream shop is a true one. I know because I was there, watching my own group of young people share God's love in their unique, special way—unplanned, unrehearsed, and completely powerful.

God can use youth as clowns. He can use them to entertain. He can use them to deliver the message of salvation. He can use them to touch lives. Unbounded opportunities await for those who are willing to serve. Is there a place for your young people in this unique ministry? You bet there is!

What does it take to start a clowning ministry? It takes one committed heart, one leader who loves to laugh and desires to share joy with the world, one person willing to learn and to explore the vast possibilities that a clowning ministry for youth has to offer. These possibilities include not only touching lives and reaching a lost world for Jesus Christ, they also reach the young people who participate in life-changing ways. And it grows from there.

1
Clowning as a Witnessing Tool for Youth

"Don't let anyone look down on you because you are young, but set an example for the believers in speech, in life, in love, in faith and in purity" (1 Tim. 4:12 NIV).

Any youth leader asked to describe the young people in his or her group would no doubt use such phrases as *boundless energy, giggling, constantly moving,* and possibly even *silly*. At times a leader sees these characteristics as the very things that interfere with a devotional time or make a youth planning meeting seem to last an eternity. God, on the other hand, uses these same qualities in constructive and effective ways to reach a lost world.

Youth can, and should, have a vital role in missions and witnessing. While their talents, spiritual development, and social skills are quite different from those of adults, there is a place for their unique abilities in God's service. They need to have opportunities to be the kind of Christian example that Paul writes about in 1 Timothy 4:12.

What better assets can teenagers offer for service than their energy, their enthusiasm, and their laughter? And what better ministry to utilize these qualities in a positive manner than clowning?

Christian clowning is a special ministry that often works well in secular settings where the more traditional methods of witnessing may not be as effective. It can provide a non-threatening environment where people are more easily approached.

With exaggerated features, bold colors, and baggy pants, a clown is an understatement of conspicuousness. He or she has only to appear on the scene and people are instinctively curious and ready to laugh. Because clowns universally represent joy and laughter, people are naturally drawn to them.

It is this automatic attraction that makes clowning such a wonderful ministry for youth. By nature, youth are very aware of self. The opinions of others, and particularly peers, matter a great deal; and to approach a total stranger and talk about Jesus . . . well, this is unthinkable for one so self-conscious!

However, a miraculous change occurs in youth when they become Christian clowns. They take on a new identity—one that fits not only into the secular scene more comfortably but also allows them to take risks to witness in a unique way without fear of personal rejection. Since people are drawn to them, youth clowns feel unconditionally accepted. They realize that it is not they themselves who are being laughed at—rather it is their clown character. They feel less threatened, and eventually even the shyest of young people can become a bold witness for Christ!

Young people constantly try to fit in, and it is important that youth leaders help them to find their place within the church and God's service. Outreach ministries are not reserved only for adults.

"Then Jesus came to them and said, 'All authority in heaven and on earth has been given to me. Therefore go and make disciples of all nations, baptizing them in the name of the Father and of the Son and of the Holy Spirit, and teaching them to obey everything I have commanded you. And surely I am with you always, to the very end of the age'" (Matt. 28:18–20 NIV).

Jesus delivered the Great Commission to His disciples, the believers. It extends to His disciples, His believers, today. And it applies to every believer—not just those of a certain age.

Christian clowning provides a place of service where youth can easily fit in. The antics and pranks of clowns provide a context in which youth can express their childishness and vent their confusion—and often frustration—in dealing with the transition from adolescence to adulthood. The spiritual cohesiveness of the ministry itself provides an atmosphere in which youth can grow as Christians, as well as offer fellowship and support to other young people.

Youth are full of ideas and seem to thrive on having an opportunity to express them. Because clowning generally does not require the memorization of speaking parts and allows freedom of physical movement, it is less confining than more traditional dramas and gives youth a means of self-expression. Of course, temper this expression with some amount of adult supervision! Clowning practice sessions provide times for youth to work out aggressions, act their silliest, and try new feats.

Encourage them to do so. However, in order to meet the needs of people in any particular ministry setting and to assure that actions of the youth do not detract from the message of the ministry, establish parameters of good taste and timing before you actually present a program. Use practice times to meet the needs of youth, but use program times to meet the needs of others.

Of course, youth want to have fun and laugh. The contagious laughter of an enthusiastic leader encourages youth. It helps them to disregard the negative perception of being laughed at and creates in them a desire to invoke laughter in others. Clowning is a relaxing, enjoyable experience for those clowning as well as for those watching. In fact, the key to good clowning is to have fun! The more fun the clowns are having, the more fun those watching will have—and the more receptive they will be to the message.

The benefits of being part of a clowning ministry are much more far-reaching than merely meeting a few psychological needs of teenagers. Participating in such a ministry helps young people to increase their commitment to God's work as they experience firsthand the rewards of such service. They quickly learn that serving God is fun, and the joy of being in God's presence becomes a driving force in their lives. Ultimately, youth will feel more at ease offering a witness to friends, neighbors, and others even without a clown disguise.

By watching and recognizing God's work through their efforts, youth become more apt to see God at work in other ways. A well-planned clowning ministry that includes spiritual development opens the eyes of youth to the abundance of witnessing opportunities that surround them each day. As they begin to rely on the Holy Spirit, and as they are encouraged in faith through their involvement with a clowning ministry, youth become more aware of these opportunities and more willing to take them.

WHAT IS CHRISTIAN CLOWNING?

"We are fools for Christ" (1 Cor. 4:10 NIV).

As Christians we are already marked as "fools" by the world. This is not to say that the gospel we believe is a joking matter or that we do foolish things. Because our Christian ideals and lifestyles do not fit the norm of a worldly society, they seem foolish to people who have not yet comprehended the saving grace of Jesus Christ. A clowning ministry helps these people see and accept the truth of the gospel through humor and laughter.

Secular clowning has been around for centuries. Christian clowning has been a viable means of reaching people for Christ since the 1970s and 1980s and has continued to grow in popularity. As ministers, clowns present life's problems in ridiculous ways and then offer Jesus Christ as the solution. They express the truths of the Bible in an exaggerated manner that not only entertains but also makes a lasting impression.

There are several marked differences between clowning as an entertainment medium and clowning as a Christian ministry. For secular clowns, the performance is the goal and also the reward. For Christian clowns, revealing Jesus Christ is the goal and sharing in God's joy is the reward.

Two nationally known clown ministers share their ideas about the purpose of Christian clowning:

"The goal of a Christian clown is to provide an avenue for the Holy Spirit to use in directing and bringing people to a closer personal relationship with Jesus Christ. Clowning is a tool that can be used to minister to the needs of people regardless of their age or the color of their skin."—Billy Don Roberts[1]

"Our purpose as silent clowns is to go out and show God's love without speaking or any means of written communication. So what do we do? We do what the New Testament tells us to do. We care; we share; we reach out and touch."—Holice Turnbow[2]

Clowning as a Christ-centered ministry is not done for performance' sake. The clowns are not performers; rather they are ministers reaching out to those with whom they come in contact. It is important, however, to practice techniques and skits—God calls us to offer our best. Practicing techniques and skits makes a difference in how well a clowning ministry holds the attention of its audience. Not all clowning programs are presented in church buildings or confined areas. Many opportunities arise in large, crowded areas such as parks, festivals, and malls, where the clowns' skills are critical in attracting and holding the attention of an audience. Although a good performance is important, the primary concern is always ministry.

A clown ministry must also discern the fine line between fantasy and reality. **Christian clowns must ensure that the reality of the gospel is not confused with the fantasy of bright-colored clowns—particularly when dealing with small children.** Older children and adults are able to discern that a clown is merely a person in costume and makeup. Smaller children may not be able to make that distinction.

Everett Robertson offers these suggestions in his book, *The Ministry of Clowning*:

1. Clowns can present the plan of salvation, but they must never extend an invitation to children to make a decision for Christ. The clown is a character of fantasy, but the gospel is very real. The young child may make a decision based on the beautiful clown . . . not on an understanding of Christ.

2. Never let clowns lead in prayer with young children. Again, the child may associate prayer, which is real, with the clown, which is not.

3. Clowns cannot give a testimony of their character's salvation experience. They are not real and can never be saved. However, the clown can, of course, give his personal testimony. Be certain the child discerns the difference between the clown and his character.[3]

To prevent portraying the gospel message as clowning fantasy, take these two simple steps. First, keep at least one member of the clowning troupe out of costume and available to talk with children or adults who have questions. Second, be prepared for instances when a clown will need to pray with a child. When such situations arise, the clown should remove his or her wig, plastic nose, hat, etc., to indicate that he or she is coming out of the clown character (fantasy) in order to pray (reality).

In summary, Christian clowning invokes the skills, techniques, and paraphernalia of secular clowning to instill in the hearts of its ministers a desire to reveal Jesus Christ rather than merely to entertain. Clown minister Buddy Lamb cites Smalley and Trent's book, *The Blessing*, in suggesting ways Christian clowns can be a blessing to others:

- **Through a meaningful touch.** A gentle touch often offers more encouragement than words. We must break down emotional walls.

- **Through a spoken word.** Christian clowns speak both through words and through actions as they communicate care and love. What they say with their bodies is as important as what they say with their lips.

- **By attaching great worth.** A Christian clown sees all individuals as persons of worth simply because God loves them.

- **By instilling hope.** Laughter brings hope. It can momentarily relieve pain and provide a reason to see a better future.

- **By having an active commitment.** Christian clowns must be committed to what they are doing and allow God to use them.[4]

---

[1] Everett Robertson, comp., *The Ministry of Clowning* (Nashville: Broadman Press, 1983), 8.
[2] Ibid., 12.
[3] Ibid., 8.
[4] Buddy Lamb, comp., *Clown Scripts for Churches* (Nashville: Convention Press, 1991), 8–9.

3
ORGANIZING A CLOWNING MINISTRY FOR YOUTH

"May he give you the desire of your heart and make all your plans succeed" (Psalm 20:4 NIV).

The task of planning and organizing any youth ministry can seem overwhelming, especially to new youth leaders. Jesus Himself demonstrated how to plan for overwhelming tasks (Mark 6:35–44). With a scant five loaves of bread and only two fish, Jesus was able to satisfy the hunger of over 5,000 people. This act was nothing less than a miracle. The method of this miracle demonstrates a practical plan for overcoming difficult tasks.

"His disciples . . . said . . . 'Send the people away so they can go to the surrounding countryside and villages and buy themselves something to eat.' But he [Jesus] answered, 'You give them something to eat'" (Mark 6:35–37 NIV).

Identify the need and the task. The disciples already recognized a need. The hour was getting late and the crowd had been listening to Jesus teach for most of the day. Perhaps one of the disciples heard his own stomach begin to growl. Perhaps the aroma of fresh bread wafted up from the village below. Regardless of what prompted the revelation, the disciples recognized the need: hunger. They even offered a plan of their own as the solution. Jesus too acknowledged the need, but the plan He offered was not what the disciples expected. Rather it was one that would have an eternal impact for thousands on the hillside that day, satisfying far more than merely their physical hunger.

As Christians we also recognize a need in our world: the need of lost people to hear and receive the gospel of Jesus Christ. Like the disciples, we often offer our own plans to meet this need. Jesus' solution may not be what we expect. But when we follow wholeheartedly, we too can be part of something that will have an eternal impact on the world.

"They said to him, 'That would take eight months of a man's wages! Are we to go and spend that much on bread and give it to them to eat?'" (Mark 6:37 NIV).

Recognize that the task is overwhelming. What Jesus asked seemed impossible to the disciples. And the task was, indeed, more than they themselves could handle. They had to trust God.

To a youth leader, developing a clowning ministry not only will, but *should*, seem overwhelming. Tasks that are more than we can handle cause us to rely on God for strength. If you believe God is calling you into the ministry of clowning with youth, you have to trust Him.

"'How many loaves do you have?' he asked. 'Go and see.' When they found out, they said, 'Five—and two fish'" (Mark 6:38 NIV).

Take stock of your resources. Jesus instructed the disciples to take stock of their resources. He did not ask them to see if they had *enough* loaves. He did not ask them to see how big those loaves were. He asked them to see what they had, regardless of whether or not they thought it would get the job done. And when the disciples had taken stock, they reported to Jesus what they found.

What do you have in the way of resources for a clowning ministry? Time? Energy? An attic full of prop possibilities? Financial resources? Dramatic abilities? Sign language skills? A love for humor and laughter? Go and take stock. Then report to Jesus. He is not interested in how much of a particular resource you have. Jesus just wants you to take stock, to recognize what you *do* have, and then to acknowledge to Him what you find.

"Then Jesus directed them to have all the people sit down in groups on the green grass. So they sat down in groups of hundreds and fifties" (Mark 6:39-40 NIV).

Break the task down into manageable parts. Jesus helped the disciples overcome their anxiety about a seemingly impossible task by breaking it down into more manageable parts. Imagine how much more manageable a group of 50 or 100 people seemed to a disciple who had looked earlier at a group of over 5,000!

As you consider the challenge of developing a youth clowning ministry, break it down into manageable parts. To focus on the whole picture before you are ready could dissuade you from the task altogether. Focus on one manageable part at a time. As you make progress, you will see results and learn to trust God with each subsequent step.

"Taking the five loaves and the two fish and looking up to heaven, he gave thanks and broke the loaves. Then he gave them to his disciples to set before the people. He also divided the two fish among them all. They all ate and were satisfied, and the disciples picked up twelve basketfuls of broken pieces of bread and fish. The number of the men who had eaten was five thousand" (Mark 6:41–44 NIV).

Give yourself and your resources to God with thanksgiving. By human standards it would have been impossible to feed over 5,000 people with only five loaves and two fish. But Jesus took those limited resources; thanked God for providing them; and offered them to God, trusting in Him to meet the need with what was offered. And because the offering was made unselfishly and with a desire to do God's will, God blessed it and the people were fed with 12 basketfuls left over!

If we look at our resources, our talents, or our abilities by human standards, they too may appear severely inadequate. But when we take those same resources, thank God for them, and offer them unselfishly and with a desire to glorify God, He will bless them just as He did the loaves and the fish. What appear to be limited resources will not only meet the need, but will provide leftovers as well!

The need and God's call to the task have been identified: You wish to use a clowning ministry to reveal Jesus Christ to a world of lost people. The task seems overwhelming; it requires God's strength and help. You have taken stock of the resources at hand and have offered them with thanksgiving to God for His use and His glory. Now you are ready to begin work on those manageable parts that will ultimately lead to a successful clowning ministry.

One of the best features of a clowning ministry is that it can start small. You need not incorporate all aspects of clowning into a ministry at the very beginning. In fact, it is better that you do not. Chances are that a clowning ministry leader will be as new to clowning as the youth they are to lead. As leaders and youth learn together, slow and steady steps will bring more success than a muddled attempt to "do it all at once."

You have taken the first step. You have determined that God may be leading your youth into a clowning ministry and have accepted the task. The second step is prayer. Make prayer a constant activity throughout the organization and duration of a clowning ministry. Where do you go from there?

1. Determine interest.

Do not spend a great amount of time learning about clowning and purchasing skit booklets if your youth are not interested in this ministry. A youth in a clowning ministry who truly does not want to be there can destroy the witnessing potential of the entire group. Do not assume that all your youth will want to be part of a clowning ministry. Limit participation to those who are.

If there is another clowning ministry active in your area, invite them to present a workshop or demonstration for your youth. Watching another group having fun with clowning and being able to ask questions one-on-one builds interest as well as generates ideas.

2. Learn and make plans.

Any youth leader who dares lead a youth session without preparing ahead of time is asking for problems! It is hard enough to keep a group of youth on track when a solid plan is in place, much less without one.

First, learn about clowning yourself. This learning process continues as you acquire additional resource materials, observe other clown ministers, and share ideas. Make frequent visits to the local library and read books about clowning and pantomime. Learn about different types of clowns; discover the techniques of basic clowning skills; explore new realms such as balloon sculpturing, juggling, or perhaps sign language. As you progress in this learning experience, you will discover your own personal interests. These personal interests will generate your own enthusiasm and will be the logical first learning experiences for your youth. It is always easier to be enthusiastic about something you are interested in personally. As a leader, your enthusiasm is essential to generate and maintain interest in this fledgling ministry.

The next task is to plan—not the details, but an overview of the ministry, its goals, and how you will accomplish those goals. Seek out resources for costumes, makeup, prizes, balloons, and skits. Begin a card file of contact persons and/or agencies that are potential target groups for the ministry in your community. Talk with your pastor or minister of youth about the possibilities for a clowning ministry and set aside specific times and places for the ministry to meet.

3. Know your role as director.

Many responsibilities fall on the shoulders of the director of a clowning ministry. Share these responsibilities with other adult leaders or delegate to responsible youth. Some youth might not want to be a clown in the ministry but may want to help in leadership or behind-the-scenes roles. Encourage these youth in their commitment and tap into their particular talents and abilities.

In general, the responsibilities of a clowning ministry director include:

- **Spiritual leadership**. In order to maintain a Christ-centered ministry, provide spiritual leadership for the youth. Begin each meeting or practice session with a time of devotion and prayer. In addition, plan special meetings to train youth in personal witnessing skills or to provide related Bible studies to increase missions awareness and the need for outreach.

- **Training**. The director is responsible for the training of other leaders as well as the youth. This is an ongoing learning process and an area in which the director may feel unqualified. Rest assured that no clown minister or director started out knowing all there is to know about clowning. In fact, that is impossible, as the craft is constantly changing! A director teaches as he or she learns. Begin with the basics and add the extras as the ministry matures. Once your group masters the basics, clowning becomes merely a matter of finding and practicing skits, building a collection of props, planning programs, and enhancing the ministry as it grows.

- **Communications.** The director must notify ministry members of all practice times and special meetings as well as program dates. He or she should compile a list of possible contacts in the community and arrange for the first several programs for the group. The director also communicates with appropriate church staff members so that practice and program schedules do not conflict with other church or youth activities.

- **Budget**. Will the ministry be financed through the church or youth budget? A clowning ministry with a church large enough to support the program with a budget is truly blessed! If each youth purchases his or her own makeup, supplies, and costume, you can keep the cost of the ministry at a minimum, with transportation, props, and music the only major items to consider. The director must determine how the ministry will be financed and take steps to make the best utilization of available resources.

- **Supplies**. The director is responsible for ordering supplies such as makeup, prizes, face painting materials, balloons, etc., depending on the needs of the ministry.

- **Transportation**. How are the clowning group, equipment, and props to be transported from one place to another? Are church vans available or are personal cars needed? The director must determine how and how often the ministry will travel into the community and how far they will be able to go.

- **Storage space**. While each youth is responsible for storing and taking care of his or her own makeup supplies and costume, plan to provide storage space for props, balloons, prizes, etc. Ideally, space is provided at the church close to the area where the ministry practices so that props and supplies are easily accessed. The director works with other church leaders to secure storage space for the clowning ministry.

- **Practice space**. Try to secure a fellowship hall or large room with a high ceiling for clowning practice. A large space allows room for expression by the youth and reduces disasters with props. The director schedules the use of church space as well as setup and cleanup before and after each session.

- **Publicity**. When the ministry is ready to take its first step out into the community, the director contacts appropriate agencies or individuals to schedule programs or activities. Chances are that word-of-mouth advertising will provide the best publicity for the ministry. However, as the group matures and is ready to take on a more expanded schedule, consider brochures, announcements in denominational newsletters, or flyers.

- **Programs**. Whether the director initiates the contact or the contact is made directly to the church, dates and times for programs need to be set. Youth schedules are hectic ones—particularly during the school year. Consider these when scheduling clowning programs. Set a date and time for a program, then check with the clowns themselves before making a firm commitment. The flexibility of the ministry is critical to its survival. If a full group of eight to ten clowns is not available, perhaps the same program will work equally as well with fewer.

- **Evaluation.** As a clowning ministry spreads its wings and tries new skits, new activities, and new skills, it needs to be evaluated. What type of program seemed to work best with the youth? What one-on-one activities were most effective with children? With youth? With adults or the elderly? Does the format for the ministry's organization need to be changed in any way? What new ideas have you gleaned that you can incorporate into the ministry for next year? A good time for such evaluation is at the end of the year, just prior to an annual enlistment period. Include some or all of the youth members of the group as well as other leaders in evaluating the strengths and weaknesses of the ministry. Avoid criticizing any facet of the ministry; focus on strengths and ways to improve the overall ministry.

4. Enlist leaders and members.

Ideally, a clowning ministry has several adult leaders. However, responsible youth can take on many of the leadership roles. Building leadership skills is a valuable by-product of a clowning ministry.

The size of a clowning ministry depends on the number of interested youth and available adult leadership. Such a ministry can be effective with only one clown. Or a group of six to eight works well.

A group larger than eight to ten can become cumbersome for several reasons. It is impossible to keep all youth in a larger clowning group busy at the same time during practice. Ordinarily, only two to five youth are involved in practicing a particular skit, leaving several others to sit idly by. With nothing tangible to occupy their time, this naturally leads to talking, getting off track, and losing interest. This leads to disruption. In addition, transportation problems are more likely with a larger group.

If a large number of youth are interested in participating in the ministry, consider enlisting additional leaders and forming two or more smaller groups. While a larger group is not impossible to work with, a smaller size is more effective and more easily managed.

Once a clowning ministry begins working together, it is advisable not to add new clowns until the following year. One reason for this is that the group begins to gel, developing clown characters that mesh to form a unified community of personalities. Also, once a group learns the basic clowning techniques and is ready to move on to the business of skits and other clowning skills, it is difficult to bring in new youth who do not yet possess these abilities.

Set an enlistment time each year to allow new groups to form or to add new members to an existing group. Such a procedure helps build interest in the ministry, giving youth an exciting activity to look forward to. Avoid tryouts. Encourage all youth interested in the ministry to participate.

Because a clowning ministry is an outreach activity and because these youth will represent your church and Jesus Christ, consider some requirements for membership.

- Ask all members to share their own personal testimony. This is critical to a Christ-centered ministry. While clowning is fun, it is a serious witnessing tool as well. Each member and leader in the ministry needs to have a personal testimony and be trained and prepared to share it.

- Require members to be active in the church youth group (or youth missions organization) for at least one year before joining the clowning ministry and remain active during the time they are part of the ministry. Commitment to Christ must come before commitment to clowning.

- Require all members to attend an initial clowning workshop. (Prior to enlisting members for the year, conduct a clowning workshop during which interested youth can learn the basics of clowning, makeup, skits, and how to use clowning as a witnessing tool. A suggested outline for a basic clowning workshop for youth is in appendix B.)

- Require members to attend all practices and programs.

- Require members to provide their own costume and makeup kit. (You can order professional Clown White and greasepaints in bulk, but make each person responsible for supplying other makeup needs. A list of items needed for a basic makeup kit is included in chap. 5.)

- Ask all members to exhibit behavior that reflects a positive attitude and a Christian spirit at all practices and programs as well as in their everyday lives. Lifestyle witnessing becomes extremely important when young people become members of a clowning ministry. Their personal daily witness must be consistent with the witness they portray as part of the clowning ministry.

5. Provide training.

Training is an ongoing activity beginning with an explanation of the purpose and objectives of the clowning ministry. Motivate and encourage members to use clowning as a means to reveal Jesus Christ—not merely as a form of entertainment.

Target basic clowning techniques next in a training program. Incorporate these into all skits and one-on-one activities. While each skit is different, the various clowning skills employed are basically the same.

Skits are the mainstay of a clowning ministry. These short pieces of pantomime or drama are the tools of communicating joy and of revealing God's love and salvation. As each new skit is presented for practice, encourage youth to try various roles until they find one that seems to suit their clown character best. Trying new skits will not only increase the ministry's repertoire, but will also allow youths' clown characters to develop.

As the ministry grows, and you find you need more and more one-on-one activities, spend some practice and training time working on special skills such as balloon sculpturing, juggling, sign language, etc. These are fun activities and will vary the practice schedule to keep it interesting. Even juggling is just a matter of practice . . . or so the experts say! Balloon sculpturing and basic sign language are fairly easy to learn and can be effective clowning tools.

Training youth to minister and witness as clowns is a multifaceted task. Each young person brings at least one unique talent to the ministry. These talents can range from riding a unicycle to being a good listener, or from possessing a compassionate heart to having gymnastic abilities.

It is the job of the clowning leader to identify the talents of each youth and to encourage those particular talents through the ministry. A young person who can juggle may or may not feel comfortable speaking openly with others. On the other hand, a young person who has no problem at all gently touching the hand of an elderly woman or conversing with a mentally handicapped person may be a complete physical klutz! Identify the strengths of each youth and use them. Nurture and encourage youth to use their talents and abilities for Christ. A lifestyle of witnessing is a natural outcome of this process.

Part of the clowning ministry training is to teach youth to respond to the needs of specific target groups such as the elderly, physically or mentally handicapped persons, persons in family crisis, the economically disadvantaged, and so forth. Before any program is presented, spend time discussing the needs of the particular target group scheduled to receive the program and how the clowning ministry can meet those needs.

For example, the needs of children in a resort setting might include the desire to feel important and loved. Parents often wish to have time for themselves while on vacation and children may feel unwanted. Youth clowns can make these children feel important and loved with one-on-one activities such as face painting or balloon sculpturing following a program of skits. Witnessing can take place simply by starting a conversation with, "Did you like the clowns? Which skit was your favorite?" If one of the message skits is mentioned, the clown can retell the message to the child. If not, the youth clown might say, "I like that one too. Another one of my favorites is [*name the message skit*] because it helps me to remember that God loves us." Face painting or balloon sculpturing are tools that hold a child's attention so that youth can give a short conversational witness.

In the situation of a nursing home or hospital, physical touch becomes extremely important. The elderly especially enjoy the touch of a hand on theirs, a hug, or a pat of reassurance. And they, in turn, like to touch others. Youth need to be trained to be accustomed to this behavior and to be willing to lean down to a stroke victim in a wheelchair and treat him or her as normally as they would a physically well person. In this case, they give a witness through love in action.

6. Keep records and maintain contact.

As the clowning ministry begins, contact community agencies or church and civic leaders to schedule programs. Once the ministry becomes active within the community, however, word-of-mouth promotion will no doubt keep the group busy. Keep records of each location a program is presented and which skits were used. This way, return visits to a particular site will not duplicate skits a second or third time around!

Yes, undertaking leadership of a youth clowning ministry *is* an overwhelming task. There is extensive learning and a multitude of details involved. One must find the extra time and muster the surplus energy. To say there will not be times of aggravation, frustration, and even total confusion would be misleading. The rewards, however, are immeasurable, the joys are unbounded, and the changed lives are definitely worth the journey!

CLOWNING BASICS

"Let the wise listen and add to their learning, and let the discerning get guidance" (Prov. 1:5 NIV).

In order to attract and hold the attention of the audience, a clown must be more than a person in baggy pants and makeup. His or her character must have substance. This substance comes through learning, practicing, and developing basic techniques.

"We each have a little clown inside us, waiting to pop out and express itself in a romantic and fun way. . . . This doesn't mean you simply put on makeup and a costume and jump around in an inspired 'clown frenzy.' Clown is a serious art form, and you need to approach it in a disciplined and systematic manner."[1]

Clowning is not a talent, it is a technique. And anyone can learn a technique. A person cannot *be* a clown; he or she must *become* a clown. Clowning is a continual process of disciplined learning that requires practice and commitment. Through this process, youth can *become* clowns. Personalities that belong only to their clown characters begin to emerge. A transformation occurs each time youth adorn their makeup and costume, taking on a whole new nature. The time youth spend at practice sessions improving basic clowning techniques and skills helps them to discover their "clown within."

At first, a youth's attempts at clowning may appear to be more akin to overacting than the execution of controlled, exaggerated movements. As they become accustomed to (and even learn to enjoy) being laughed at and begin to feel at ease with the basic clowning skills, more and more of their individual clown character traits begin to surface. Some clown characters are naturals for comic or slapstick routines. Others are more adept at message skits. Several are equally comfortable in either area. A well-rounded clowning ministry is comprised of a variety of clown personalities.

The object of clowning is not to draw attention to the clown but rather to draw attention to the action. Wes McVicar puts it this way:

"The clown is a medium, and the audience is not so interested in who the clown is, as in what he does and how he does it."[2]

An exception does exist for Christian clowns, however. In one-on-one witnessing situations, the clown himself or herself is most important, as is the individual spirit of the clown that conveys God's love—not props or comic actions. During clowning skits and programs, though, an individual's personality must take a back seat to the action to ensure that the clown does not overshadow the message.

The Basics

The basics of clowning can be grouped into four major areas: (1) pantomime, (2) showing emotions, (3) exaggerating movements and actions, and (4) connecting with an audience.

Pantomime

The art of pantomime in clowning originated as circus clowns found themselves in large performance areas with no type of amplification, and their voices simply could not be heard. They had to use gestures to communicate action; and because gesture is a universal language, they were easily understood.

In its most basic form, "*mime* is the expression or communication of an emotion, a thought, an idea, or a story through body gestures and facial expressions, and without any spoken words."[3] Pure mime uses no props—all objects as well as actions and emotions are communicated through gestures.

Mastering the skills of pantomime is a tedious task for youth who are anxious to participate in clowning skits as soon as possible. Mime is an exacting skill that requires a great deal of time to acquire. For this reason and because of the more self-conscious nature of youth, you may want to use props to clearly identify objects. While most objects may be portrayed with props, all actions, attitudes, feelings, and emotions are shown through pantomime, or gesturing.

Showing Emotions

One universal characteristic of clowns is that they show emotion and show it in undeniable ways. Changing emotions frequently, they may move from happiness to sadness to utter fear to anger and back to happiness again all within the same short skit. Most clowning is done without verbal communication, and a clown must convey exactly how he or she feels without using words. Since the purpose of any well-executed skit is for the audience to relate to the clown's predicament, clowns must learn the essential technique of showing emotion in such a way as to make the audience feel those same emotions.

Showing emotion involves the entire body. While the face is the focal point, gestures added with arms, legs, and body movement help to convey the depth of a particular feeling or attitude. For example, a sorrowful face might tell an audience that a clown is sad; but that same face along with a quivering jaw, heaving shoulders, or the wiping of tears tells them just how deep the sadness is. Or a look of apprehension might tell an audience that a clown is nervous; but the chewing of fingernails (perhaps in typewriter roll fashion), the wiping of perspiration from a forehead followed by the wringing out of a handkerchief, and the uncontrollable wobbling of knees lets the audience know the intensity of that emotion.

To train youth to express their emotions, encourage them to practice facial expressions in front of a mirror. As their clown characters develop, it becomes easier for them to add body movement and gestures to emphasize intensity. Another exercise is to encourage youth to spend some time each day making themselves aware of their emotions and how often those emotions change. In a suitable environment (preferably at home and not a school classroom!), they should practice expressing each emotion they feel in an exaggerated style. During family dinnertime, for example, they can express emotions as the family discusses the business of the day. As a brother talks about scoring the winning basket in the afternoon's game, the youth clown could express anticipation, excitement, joy, and pride. As a younger sister tells about being chased by a neighborhood dog, the youth clown might express disbelief, anxiety, fear, concern, and relief that the child returned home safely.

Whatever the training exercise, it is important that youth learn to recognize their emotions and to feel free to show them. Remind youth often that a clown's emotions are expressed with the whole body and not just through facial expressions.

Some basic emotions and their degrees of intensity to practice are:
- happiness (from gentle joy to sheer bliss)
- sadness (from disappointment to wailing sobs)
- love (from flirtatious to overbearing)
- anger (from mild exasperation to boiling mad)
- nervousness (from slight anxiety to uncontrollable panic)
- irritation (from slightly annoyed to completely infuriated)
- sleepiness (from slightly drowsy to dead on your feet)
- cold (from feeling a sudden cool breeze to freezing)
- hot (from mild discomfort to searing desert heat)
- surprise (from a pleasant surprise to a terrifying one)

Clowning skits can utilize any number of emotions, and a clown must move easily from one to another yet maintain some type of expression at all times. Take the simple action of eating an ice-cream cone. Suppose a clown is excited and happy at the anticipation of eating the delicious treat; but just as his tongue touches the scoop, the ice cream rolls off the cone and onto the floor.

Using this example, imagine the scene with a clown who looks at his ice-cream cone and expresses happiness to the audience. Then he drops his expression, walks a few steps, and takes a lick. The ice-cream scoop rolls off the cone. He looks at the melting scoop, shakes his head in sadness, and walks away.

Now, imagine the same scene: The clown expresses his happiness and excitement completely and continuously to the point at which his tongue touches the scoop and causes it to roll off the cone. At that very instant, the clown's eyes meet those of the audience, and his expression changes to one of bewilderment. As his eyes fall and he sees the melting scoop on the floor, his expression changes again, building from unexpected disappointment to emotional sobbing.

Note the differences between these two scenes. In the first, the clown has little emotional depth. He goes through the actions, but fails to use sufficient emotions to relate to the audience. While he expresses some emotion, he does so in spurts, making it difficult for the audience to follow the action. Before the audience can identify with the situation, the skit is over and the clown has left the scene.

In the second example, the clown gives detailed attention to emotion, maintaining some type of expression throughout the scene. Making eye contact with the audience before he looks down at the melting ice cream, he makes the audience clearly aware of his predicament. As he looks down, he allows his feelings to build over several seconds, giving the audience sufficient time to identify with the predicament and to empathize with his emotions. This clown has done more than entertain; he has built a relationship.

On the following page is a simple clowning scenario you can use to practice continuous expression and basic audience contact. The exercise emphasizes feeling and expressing changing emotions. Individual clowns may interpret the scene in a variety of ways depending on their character types and how they themselves feel at any particular point in the action. While personal interpretations are encouraged, some emotions or feelings that might be expressed are shown in bold type and actions that might be employed are shown in italics.

FLYING BY

Number of clowns: One

Props needed: Chair (representing a park bench)
Comics section from the newspaper
Large handkerchief tucked in clown's pocket

A clown carrying a newspaper (the comics section, of course!) enters a beautiful park and is **overcome with joy** at the splendor of the area. He takes several deep breaths of the fresh air. Ah, life is grand! *(The clown smiles at the audience and indicates that he hears chirping birds. He clasps his hands in serene joy and/or simply sighs visibly.)* Still smiling, he spots a park bench *(Looks at the bench, then to the audience, pointing to the bench to draw attention to it)*, pulls a handkerchief from his pocket, and dusts off a spot before taking a seat. What a beautiful, calm place to read the day's comics. *(The clown snaps his newspaper open, making lots of crinkling noises as he finds the correct page.)*

Wait! What's this? *(The newspaper is slowly lowered to reveal the clown's eyes, his expression changing immediately from peaceful serenity to slight irritation.)* The clown is rather **annoyed** at a fly that has started buzzing around him. Carefully watching the movement of the fly *(Rolling of eyes and slight movement of head as if following the flight pattern of a buzzing insect)*, he slowly rolls up the newspaper, preparing for the kill.

The clown makes his move, lashing out at the flying menace. **Rats!** Missed. Missed again. That fly is not going to ruin his day in the park! Now, he is **more determined than ever to get that fly.**

(The clown rolls the newspaper even tighter; pushes up his sleeves; purses his lips and narrows his eyes; and might even shuffle his feet as a bull preparing to charge.)

The clown charges toward the fly, swatting wildly. Suddenly, he realizes that the fly has disappeared. *(The action stops and the clown looks bewildered and skeptical.)* He can't hear the fly *(Cups hand to ear to listen)*. He doesn't see the fly *(Looks around slowly then does a double-take quick turn to check behind himself)*. Finding no evidence of the fly buzzing around, the clown is clearly the victor. Strutting like a **proud** peacock and with a **lilt of his head** and a **sly smile** on his lips, he walks **confidently** back to the bench, snaps out his newspaper, takes his seat, and begins to read once again.

After a few seconds, the newspaper is slowly lowered revealing the clown's face. Uh-oh. He hears something *(Cups hand to ear and then starts following with his eyes the flight pattern of the buzzing fly again)*. Oh, no! That troublesome fly has returned. The clown's **anger** starts to build. *(The clown's eyes narrow; his hands start shaking the newspaper; his breathing gets heavier. He carefully rolls up the newspaper—all the while keeping his eye on the fly.)* Just as the clown is aimed and ready to swat at the fly, lo and behold it lands on his nose! *(The clown traces the fly's flight pattern with the rolled newspaper following the fly straight to his own nose and ends up cross-eyed.)* Without stopping to think, he quickly swats himself square on the nose! Ouch! That was **painful** *(Grabs nose in agony, drops paper, jumps around in pain)*. Finally, **disgusted** with the way his day is going, the clown **angrily** grabs up his newspaper and leaves in a huff, wiping the remaining pieces of the squashed fly from the tip of his nose.

Exaggerating Movements and Actions

The elements of any skit involve conveying emotions through a series of precise movements or actions. To be convincing, a clown reacts to his or her circumstances with a combination of distinguishable, overstated emotions and slow, exaggerated movements.

The reason for this exaggeration is twofold. First of all, it is the trademark of a good clown. Secondly, and more practically, the audience may be watching from a distance. A clown exaggerates his or her movements and expressions in order to be seen and understood.

In addition to being exaggerated, all movements need to be executed at a slower speed than normal. If a clown makes an action too quickly, an audience could easily miss it; and if that action is an essential part of a skit, the entire message may be lost.

For example, in the previous "Flying By" scenario, the clown takes his time in building anger. His eyes find the fly first and he lets the audience in on his situation by very slowly moving his head and eyes to follow the insect's flight pattern. Only when the audience is aware of the predicament does the clown roll up the newspaper and swat the fly. Had the clown sat down and then suddenly taken the newspaper and swatted the fly, the audience might have missed the action altogether, or at best misunderstood the predicament.

Each clowning action is a series of smaller, well-orchestrated movements that should be expressed deliberately and completely. Suppose a clown wishes to pick an apple from a tree. She would not simply reach up and pluck it from the branches. Rather, she would (1) notice the apple in the tree; (2) point to the apple to make the audience aware of its presence; (3) express why she would like to have the apple (hunger); (4) approach the tree; (5) ponder the situation; (6) decide on a course of action (jumping for the apple, shaking the branches); (7) indicate her decision to the audience; (8) execute the selected course of action; (9) retrieve the apple; (10) take a bite from the apple, thus satisfying her hunger; and (11) indicate to the audience that she is satisfied with the outcome.

To simply reach up, pick an apple, and begin eating it conveys an action, but little else. By emphasizing each smaller part of the action, as just described, the clown not only conveys the action but also communicates a motive for the action, a procedure for the action, and how she feels about what she has accomplished.

Circumstances present themselves to which a clown must react. In the apple-picking scenario, the apple may hang stubbornly on the branch, forcing the clown to formulate an alternative plan to acquire it. The apple may fall and hit the clown on the head, rendering her unconscious, or causing an exaggerated level of pain and anguish. Or, the apple may contain a worm the clown discovers only after she takes the first bite.

Listed below are several pantomime actions you can use for practice. Remember to make movements at least twice as large as normal and execute these as if moving in slow motion. Break down each action into a series of deliberate movements in order to convey completely the situation to the audience. Once an action feels comfortable, explore some possibilities for *reaction*. Imagine a circumstance and respond to it in an exaggerated fashion. Suggestions for reactions are shown below in italics.

- driving a car with a stick shift (*and the gearshift gets stuck in reverse*)
- opening a stuck window (*and a bee comes flying in*)
- balancing a plate on a stick (*and your foot gets stuck on a piece of fly paper*)
- building a campfire (*and the wind keeps blowing it out*)
- throwing a baseball (*and it's a home run hit*)
- putting on snow boots (*and after much ado realizing they are on the wrong feet*)

- playing tennis *(and continuing the game even though your pants split)*
- walking a large (or small) dog *(and a cat crosses your path)*
- painting a portrait *(and your subject will not sit still)*
- weeding a garden *(and you come across a weed that pulls back)*

The following scenario can be used to practice exaggerated movement. While the emphasis is on action, express all emotions as well. Again, different clown character types have a variety of interpretations of the scene and will react differently to the same situation. Personal interpretations are encouraged and much of the action will come from original ideas. However, a few suggested emotions or feelings that may be expressed are shown in bold type and actions that might be employed are shown in italics.

DENTAL WOES

Number of clowns: Two

Props needed: Large lollipop
Long piece of string
Piece of plastic foam packing peanut, cut to resemble a tooth
Chair

Clown 1 enters holding his jaw, **obviously suffering** from a severe toothache. *(Clown 1 enters with shoulders hunched, holding hand on jaw; eyes sullen; cringing and wincing in pain every now and then, and stopping every few steps to express the source of his pain to the audience.)* Clown 2 enters carrying a large lollipop and **obviously enjoying it.** *(Clown 2 enters, waving happily to the audience and skipping around.)* Clown 1 notices the large lollipop, and his eyes light up with **delight.** *(Still holding his jaw in his hand, Clown 1's expression changes to delightful anticipation; he straightens his stance as he spies the sweet treat.)* Clown 2 sees Clown 1 and indicates the question, Would you like a bite? *(Clown 2 points to Clown 1 and then to the lollipop with a questioning expression on his face.)* Naturally, Clown 1 **nods his head vigorously.** But as he is nodding, the **pain sharply returns** and he is reminded of his dilemma. *(As the pain returns, Clown 1 winces, grabs his jaw once again, and his shoulders quickly return to their hunched position.)* He slowly shakes his head, **pouting,** and indicates that he must **sadly** refuse the lollipop because of his toothache. *(Clown 1 pouts and lowers his head; waves his hand toward Clown 2 and the lollipop to say no; then points to his jaw and indicates the great amount of pain he is in.)*

Wait! Clown 2 has an idea! *(Clown 2 strokes his chin a few times then suddenly straightens his stance, opens his eyes wider, and holds his index finger up in the air to indicate that he has just had an idea.)* Clown 2 leads Clown 1 to a chair and helps him get seated. *(Clown 1 goes along but looks bewildered. Clown 2 behaves excitedly; brushes off the chair before seating Clown 1; situates Clown 1 just right in the chair; stands back a few steps and takes stock of the situation; then rearranges the position of Clown 1 on the chair. At last, Clown 1 is just where he needs to be.)* Now,

Clown 2 pulls some string from his pocket. *(Clown 2 reaches deep into his pocket and pulls out the string . . . and it keeps coming, and coming, and coming!)* Clown 2 approaches Clown 1 and indicates that he plans to tie the string around the bad tooth and pull it out. As Clown 2 moves closer, Clown 1 becomes **apprehensive** about the whole ordeal. *(Clown 1's eyes get wider and express anxiety; he backs up into the chair, almost crawling up into it and crouching into a fetal position; his lips are tightly closed to prevent Clown 2 from getting to the tooth.)* Clown 2 **assures** Clown 1 that he knows what he is doing. After all, he is really quite **intelligent**. Clown 1 **nervously** eases back down to a sitting position and **cautiously** opens his mouth. He can't watch this! *(Clown 1 closes his eyes tightly, peeking out every now and then.)*

Clown 2 ties the string around the tooth. *(It only appears as if the string is being tied to a tooth. Clown 1 holds the hand farthest from the audience up against his cheek—similar to the expression of pain and agony used earlier. As Clown 2 bends over to tie the string, Clown 1 holds the string tightly in his fingers. By holding the hand against the cheek, the illusion of the string being tied to a tooth inside the mouth is accomplished.)* Then, Clown 2 begins stepping away, letting out a little string as he moves along. Clown 1 still can't watch! *(More peeking.)*

One, two, three! Just as Clown 2 yanks on the string, Clown 1 bounces **anxiously** out of the chair, runs toward him, and indicates, "No, please don't do this!" Clown 2 takes Clown 1 back to the chair and reseats him, **reassuring** him that everything will be fine. Again, the string is tied onto the tooth and Clown 2 returns to his pulling spot.

One, two, three! Clown 2 yanks on the string. This time, Clown 1 has grabbed the string with his free hand and pulls back, causing Clown 2 to stumble toward the chair. Clown 2 is getting rather **irritated** and returns the yank. To which Clown 1 also yanks again. *(A short tug-of-war ensues, starting slowly with tugs, getting faster and faster, and clowns moving closer and closer together until they are nose to nose.)*

Clown 2 tries to reassure Clown 1 yet again, although he is becoming **rather annoyed** with the whole situation. He shows Clown 1 the lollipop and waves it **temptingly** in front of Clown 1's face. Clown 1 remembers now why he wanted that tooth pulled in the first place! *(Clown 1 licks his lips in anticipation.)* All right. One more time. And this time Clown 1 will not move . . . he promises. Clown 2 is somewhat **skeptical,** but once again he ties the string on the tooth. *(At this point the plastic foam packing peanut tooth is tied to the string and held in Clown 1's hand).* Clown 2 takes his end of the string and backs away slowly to a good distance.

One, two . . . pull! This time Clown 2 does not wait for the count of three! *(Clown 1 lets go of the string.)* The tooth comes flying out of Clown 1's mouth, much to his **astonishment.** *(Clown 2 looks proudly at the tooth dangling from the string, as Clown 1 grabs his face in disbelief.)*

But wait a minute! Something's not right. *(Clown 1 begins feeling around his jaw; sticks a finger inside his mouth and counts his teeth.)* Ouch! *(Clown 1 winces with pain.)* Clown 2 has pulled the wrong tooth! Now, Clown 1 is **really angry**. *(Clown 1 displays a slow, determined build of emotion, from beginning anger to absolute fury.)* Clown 2 **cautiously** offers the tooth dangling on the string back to Clown 1, who immediately chases Clown 2 offstage.

Connecting with an Audience

The fourth basic technique a clowning ministry needs to master is the art of connecting with an audience. In order for an audience to remain attentive and interested, they must become a part of the action. This is especially true in resort settings such as beach boardwalks, amusement parks, malls, etc., where an audience is transient at best. When an audience realizes that the clowns are noticing them as much as they are noticing the clowns, they are more inclined to stay and watch. Otherwise, they may lose interest and leave before receiving the spiritual message of the skit.

The best way to keep an audience's attention is by using direct and deliberate contact. In clowning, this is referred to as a *take*. A take is when, at any time during a skit, a clown stops looking at the other clowns and makes direct eye contact with a member or section of the audience. During this connection the clown either relates an emotion or a piece of vital information, shares a laugh, gives a direction, indicates a secret, or asks a question. Each routine will provide several opportunities for takes. These should occur often and be directed toward as many members of the audience as possible.

A variety of takes can be used. Begin every skit with a *greeting take*, during which you set the scene and acknowledge an audience. An *information take* indicates that some logical action is about to take place. A *devious take* signals that a clown is about to do something sneaky before the action actually transpires. A *secrecy take* usually involves touching a finger to the lips to keep an audience quiet and indicates that they are about to learn a secret about what is going to happen, where something is hidden, or who is responsible for a certain mistake. An *opinion take* involves the audience in a decision a clown is about to make. An *attitude*, or *feeling, take* occurs when a clown shares a greater intensity of an emotion or mocks another character (but never an audience member!). An *idea take* occurs naturally when a clown shares an idea with the audience.

When and where a take occurs in a skit depends on the character types of the clowns involved. An overly friendly clown may stop and use a take just to wave or smile at an audience from time to time. A devious clown would more likely use takes at times when this crafty trait is about to be exposed. A pompous clown might use takes to draw attention to his great feats by taking exaggerated bows or by encouraging applause for himself.

One word of warning: A skit may continue too long and become tiresome if it involves an overabundance of takes. A good rule to follow is to incorporate one take during the entrance of a skit (known as "greeting the audience") and two or three other major takes in the remaining sections. A quick look, a snicker, or a flash of emotion from a clown to an audience is considered a secondary take and can be used at any time.

Use the previous "Dental Woes" skit to practice, incorporating a few of the following suggested clowning takes.

A good rule to follow is to incorporate one take during the entrance of a skit (known as "greeting the audience") and two or three other major takes in the remaining sections.

Clown 1 (toothache clown). Takes 1, 3, and 4 are considered major takes; 2 is a secondary take.

Take 1: *Greeting Take.* Clown 1 greets the audience. Although the greeting is one that expresses suffering, the clown has connected directly with the audience by indicating his pain and its source. The objective is to invoke pity, set the scene, and involve the audience in the action.

Take 2: *Attitude/Feeling Take*. After the lollipop has been offered to Clown 1 and he suddenly realizes that he must decline, he indicates this disappointment directly to the audience. The objective, again, is to invoke pity, to allow the audience to empathize with the clown, and to reveal a predicament that needs to be resolved.

Take 3: *Attitude/Feeling Take*. After Clown 2 has reassured Clown 1 that he has things under control, and as Clown 2 backs away to feed out the string, Clown 1 looks directly at the audience and mouths the words, "Help me!" This can be repeated to several people or sections of the audience. The objective is to draw attention to his anxiety.

Take 4: *Attitude/Feeling Take*. As Clown 1's anger builds at the realization that the wrong tooth has been pulled, he directly faces the audience, allowing them to see the intensity of his feelings as they increase. This take is done simultaneously with take 4 listed below for Clown 2. The objective is to solidify the new predicament before any action is taken.

Clown 2 (string-pulling clown). Takes 1, 2, and 4 are major takes; 3 is a secondary take.

Take 1: *Opinion Take*. Upon seeing Clown 1 and before asking if he would like a taste of the lollipop, Clown 2 looks at the audience as if to ask if he should make the offer. The objective is to make an initial connection between Clown 2 and the audience, and to make them feel a part of the decision.

Take 2: *Idea Take*. Clown 2 gives the "I have an idea" sign to the audience as he makes plans to pull the tooth. The objective is to make the audience aware that a new idea is about to be tried before the actual action begins. This short idea take could quickly be followed with an information take, during which the clown explains to the audience that he is about to tie the string on the tooth and pull it out.

Take 3: *Devious Take*. Just before the last pull on the string (when Clown 1 pulls on the count of two instead of waiting for three), Clown 2 gives a quick look to the audience to let them know that something sneaky is about to happen.

Take 4: *Attitude/Feeling Take*. After the tooth is pulled, Clown 2 dangles the tooth in front of the audience and expresses his pride in a job well done. He may even take a few bows. This take is done simultaneously as Clown 1 realizes that the wrong tooth has been pulled.

Some youth clowns will feel more comfortable than others doing audience takes. Identify these youth and use them in the first few skits of a program to involve an audience as early as possible. Even those youth who do not feel comfortable directly confronting an audience can, in time, learn to use takes effectively and should be encouraged to try a few during each program.

When all the basic clowning techniques—pantomime, showing emotion, exaggerating movements and actions, and connecting with an audience—are combined, the result is not only entertainment but the establishment of a relationship with the audience. In a Christian clowning ministry, this relationship is essential to the one-on-one witnessing time that follows a program. Learn and practice the basics of clowning to enhance the quality of your ministry's work. This will determine how well your audience responds. While performance is not the key issue, practice is critical in sharpening the clowning skills that will make your ministry one that stands out and leaves a lasting impression.

Disciplined practice is the most effective method for learning clowning techniques. However, you can also learn a great deal by observing others gifted in the art of clowning. Examples of such skills abound and are readily available on television or videotapes. Study the exaggerated actions and facial expressions of classic cartoon characters and circus clowns; of Lucille Ball in episodes of the old *I Love Lucy* television show; of Carol Burnett, Vicki Lawrence, and Tim Conway in videotaped episodes of *The Carol Burnett Show*; or of Red Skelton's Freddy the Freeloader sketches on videotapes. Each of these has a distinct style of exaggeration and can provide stimulating ideas for youth as they develop their own clown characters.

Hold a workshop to introduce the basics of clowning and to build interest and enthusiasm for the ministry. Do this over a four-hour period to include a meal, or conduct it in two or more shorter sessions. With the basics out of the way, the ministry can then move on to learning and practicing skits that utilize and strengthen the basic techniques members have acquired.

An outline for a basic initial clowning workshop is in appendix B. Be aware that at the conclusion of the workshop, your youth will still not *be* clowns. But they will be well on their way to *becoming* clowns.

[1] Mark Stolzenberg, *Clown for Circus and Stage* (New York: Sterling Publishing Company, Inc., 1981), 7.
[2] Wes McVicar, *Clown Act Omnibus* (Colorado Springs: Meriwether Publishing Ltd., 1987), 6.
[3] Susie Kelly Toomey, *Mime Ministry* (Colorado Springs: Meriwether Publishing Ltd., 1986), 1.

Makeup and Costumes

"A cheerful look brings joy to the heart" (Prov. 15:30 NIV).

The exaggerated features and bright colors on a clown's face make it come alive. A well-designed clown face—one that matches both the personality and costume of the clown—enhances facial expression and emotion.

For the Christian clown, the process of putting on makeup is a reminder of one's hope in Jesus Christ. The white makeup applied first is a symbol of death and, in particular, it symbolizes Jesus' death on the Cross. The bold colors added to a clown's face represent the new life Jesus offers through salvation.

Types of Clowns

There are three basic types of clowns, each with a particular style of makeup and costume.

The **Whiteface clown** is one of the oldest, classic characters and is generally considered a more serious clown, often invoking sadness. Makeup for this type of clown includes covering the entire face and neck with white makeup and adding only a few markings to accentuate facial features. The costume for a Whiteface clown is ordinarily black and white, although in recent years bolder colors have come into use.

The **Tramp (or Hobo) clown** is a character that is often ridiculed or made the buffoon, usually invoking pity. The Tramp clown wears very little makeup, except dark shadows on the cheeks and chin to resemble an unshaven look and perhaps some exaggerated features around the eyes. His costume is pieced together with items such as ragged pants, an old jacket, a discarded hat, and suspenders. Colors for his costume are not bold, but rather plain and muted. This type of clown can play a character role, but is usually regarded as an outcast.

The **Auguste [oh-goost] clown** is a character of comedy involved in slapstick or more physical clowning and can invoke a wide array of emotions. This clown's makeup covers only areas around the eyes and mouth, exaggerating those features in a comical way. Rather than having a completely white face, the Auguste clown applies white makeup only to form large eyes and a mouth, then adds color for lips, nose, eyebrows, etc. The costume is flashy, using bold colors and patterns.

Makeup, Costumes, and Youth

As you survey resources on clowns and clowning, you will discover that a large variety of makeup and costume styles are available. Most of these are used by professional clowns and clown ministers—adults who intend to make longer careers of the craft than do youth, and who have the time and financial resources to create original makeup and costume designs.

For purposes of a youth clowning ministry, keep both makeup and costumes as simple and inexpensive as possible. For example, use the makeup and costume style of the Auguste clown. Use the Tramp (or Hobo) clown character also, but only one or two such characters in any one ministry.

While a youth clowning ministry should strive to be as professional as possible, consider physical comfort as well as time and financial concerns when making makeup and costume decisions. A professional clown may spend as much as an hour or longer applying his or her makeup. Youth, however, generally do not have the patience for such a lengthy endeavor. By using only exaggerated facial features rather than a complete Whiteface design, you reduce the time required for both application and removal of makeup. A completely whitefaced clown is forced not only to sport the full makeup on face and neck, but because he or she must maintain the illusion of all white skin, he or she must also add gloves and a wig to hide hands and ears. These extras add to the physical discomfort of working in outside or resort situations. With the Auguste style of makeup, you eliminate the need for wigs and gloves. Youth can create their own clown hairstyles with pigtails, braids, topknots, or ponytails adorned with brilliant-colored ribbons or bows for young women and caps or hats for young men.

The style of the Auguste clown's costume also works well with youth. Because this type of costume has a broader range of fashions, youth have more freedom in the selection of color and design to express their individuality. Not only is the Auguste clown a good choice for makeup and costume style for youth, it is also an excellent choice in character—one of humor that plays a variety of character roles. The bold costume colors and the exaggerated features of the Auguste face draw immediate attention, making this type of clown one that works well in a variety of witnessing situations—walk-arounds such as parks or malls, programs in resort areas, and one-on-one activities of all kinds.

Makeup Tips

Each member of a clowning ministry needs to learn to apply his or her own makeup. It may take several tries to discover just the right face as the youths' clown characters develop. Encourage youth to try different eye shapes, patterns, and colors until they find unique clown faces that express their personalities and match their costumes.

Regardless of which style face you select, consider the following makeup points.

1. Never put the color red directly around the eyes—this makes a clown look evil. Use white directly around the eyes. A red eyebrow placed high above the exaggerated eye or a red heart on the cheek below the eye will, however, work nicely without affecting the image of the face.

2. Never put the color blue or green around the mouth—this makes a clown look sick. Red on the lips surrounded by the contrasting white to exaggerate the feature works best.

3. Do not extend the outside edges of a clown's mouth past the outside edges of his or her *real* eyes.

4. Keep the face design simple when adding markings such as hearts, stars, freckles, eyebrows, etc. A clown's face is the focal point of his character; and emotion, even when expressed in the most professional manner, will be lost when makeup is too distracting.

Basic Makeup Supplies

Use professional greasepaint for a youth clowning ministry. This makeup maintains its color and consistency over extended periods of time both in storage and on the face. More inexpensive types of clown makeup, usually available during the Halloween season, may be tempting because of the lower price; but the extra cost of professional makeup will more than pay for itself over the long run. One small tin of Clown White and one palate of standard greasepaint colors will likely last a youth several years, while the cheaper brands will need to be replaced often.

The initial cost for a complete makeup kit will amount to approximately $20 to $25 per person. Each youth should begin putting together his or her own makeup kit to include:

- Some type of container. This can be as expensive as a new plastic organizer toolbox or as inexpensive as a shoebox. It should be large enough to hold all makeup supplies and sturdy enough to travel.
- Professional Clown White.
- Professional color palate (to include red and blue colors).
- Two black eyeliner pencils (waterproof) and a sharpener.
- Small jar of cold cream.
- Small plastic bottle to hold vegetable oil.
- Baby powder.
- Two white socks (Toes of the socks are filled with baby powder and a knot is tied about two inches from the top.).
- Large, soft-bristled makeup brush.
- Disposable makeup applicators (*not* wedge-type) or cotton swabs.
- Small plastic mist bottle for water.
- Small stand-up mirror.
- Old washcloths and handtowels.
- Optional: hairbands, colored eyeliner pencils, makeup removal pads.

Designing a Clown Face

Have youth plan their clown faces on paper before attempting to create them with makeup. Do not let them draw on their faces until they have determined the makeup design.

There are literally hundreds of variations of facial features that can be used to design a clown face. The ones shown below and on the following pages are considered the most basic, and are therefore the simplest for youth to use. As they gain experience in applying and experimenting with makeup, they can use more advanced shapes, shadings, and markings. While all youth will use basic shapes for eyes and mouths, they will add special markings to individualize faces.

The design begins by selecting a basic eye type (see below).

For youth with high foreheads, or for any who wear eyeglasses, the tall rounded or diamond shape is suggested. Those with shorter foreheads or those who wear bangs might select the short rounded or triangle eyes.

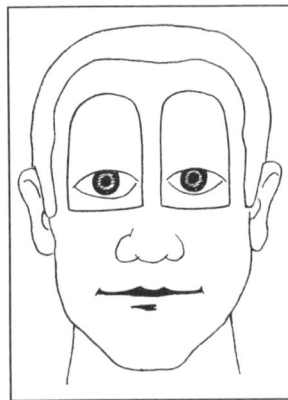 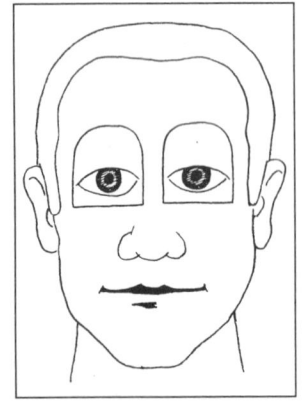 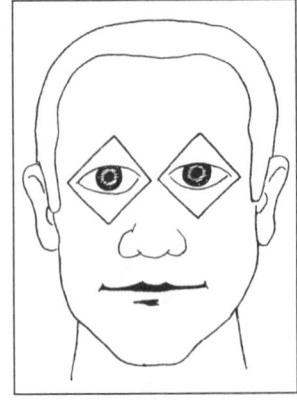 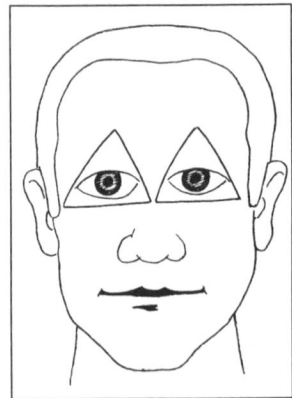

Select a style for the mouth:

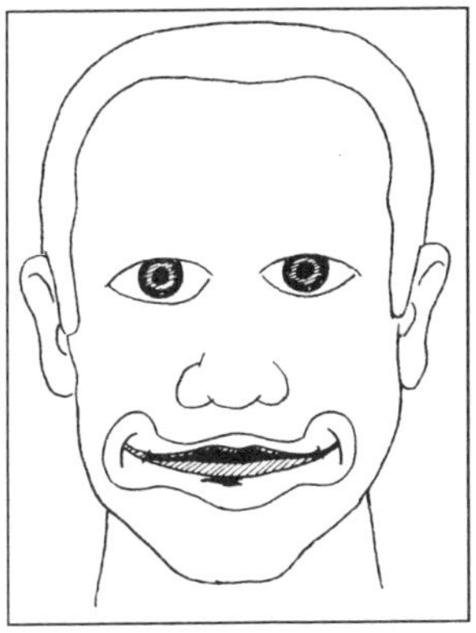

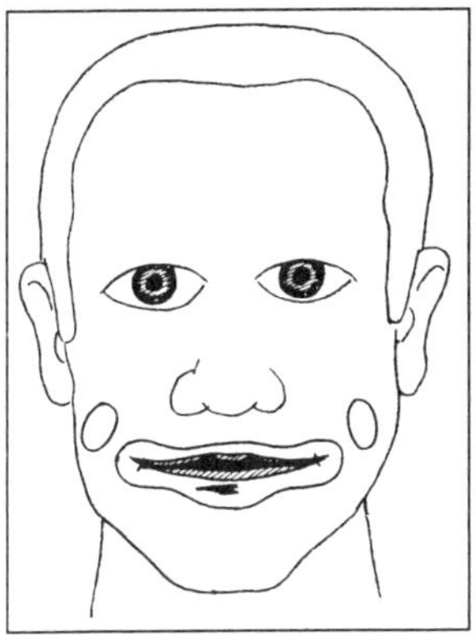

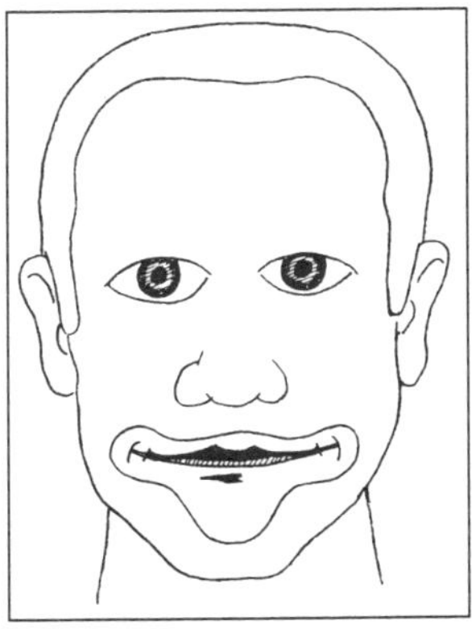

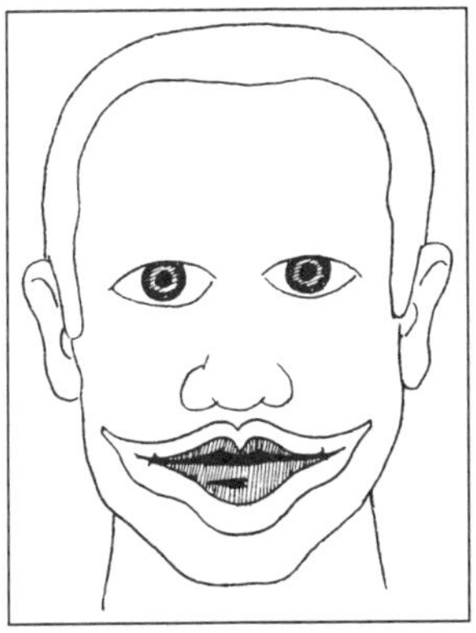

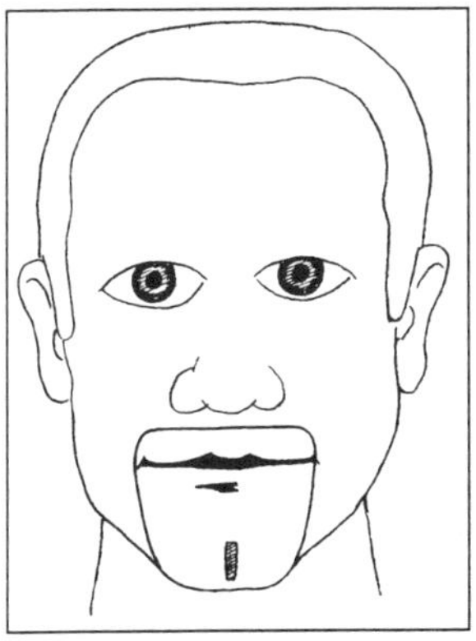

Leave the nose as is or adorn it with a simple circle, triangle, or inverted triangle:

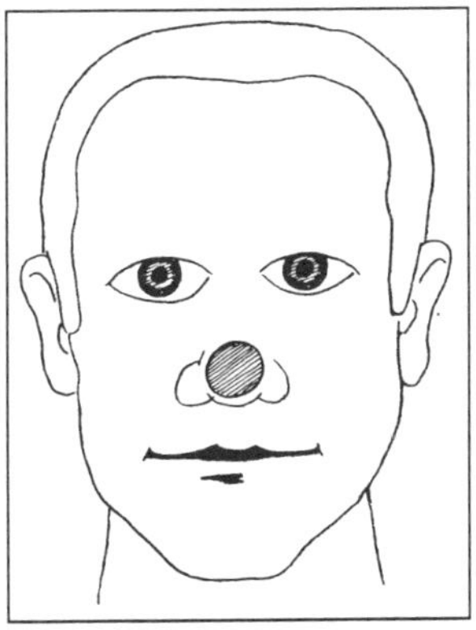

Once the basic facial features are in place, add the markings that will make each clown face unique. Add extra markings to the eyes in the form of eyebrows or accents.

Eyebrows:

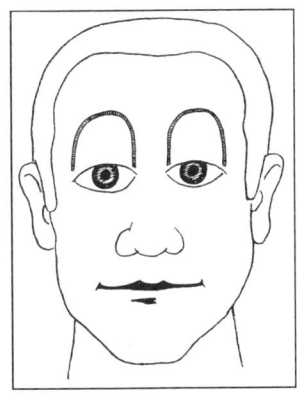 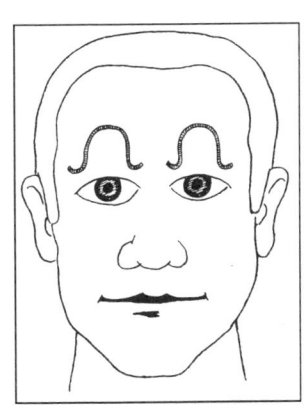 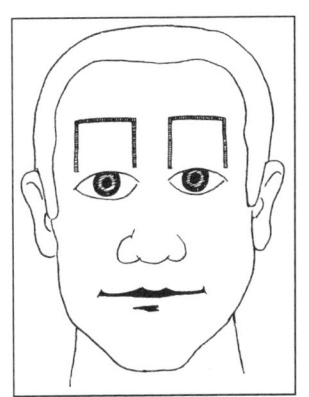 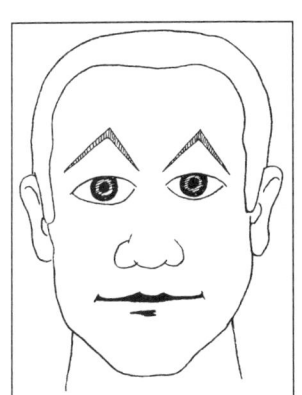

Eye Accents (usually used in lieu of eyebrows):

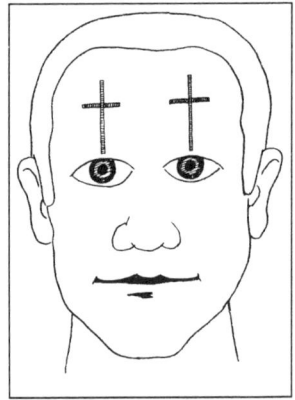 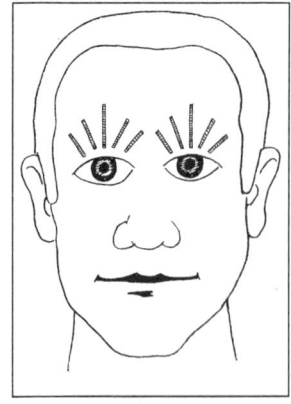 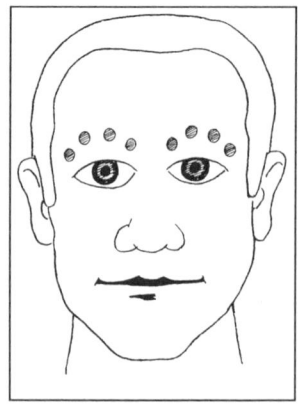 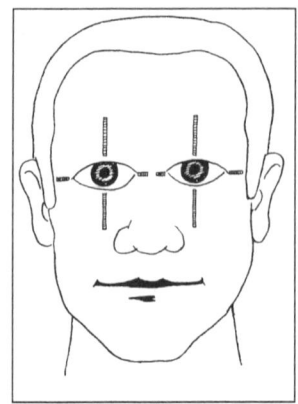

If desired, special markings can be added to the cheeks:

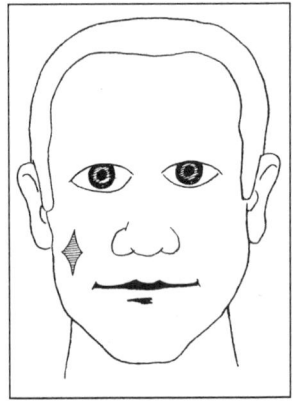 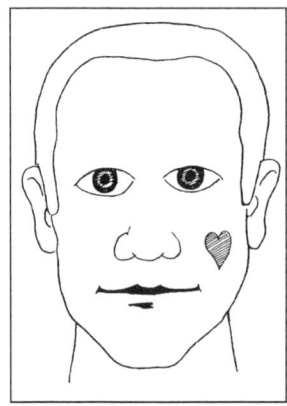 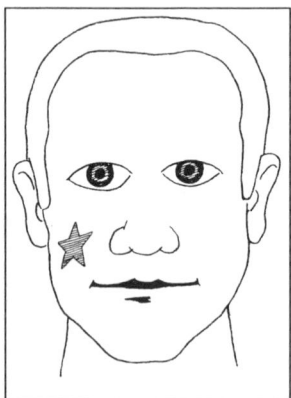 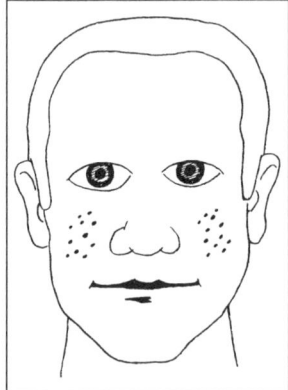

Finally, since the purpose of the ministry is to reveal Jesus Christ, use some type of Christian symbol as part of each clown's makeup. Do this by using the Christian fish symbol, either on the face or the back of one hand, or by incorporating a red circle (also a Christian symbol) within the design.

These features, and others youth might create, combine to produce a variety of unique clown faces:

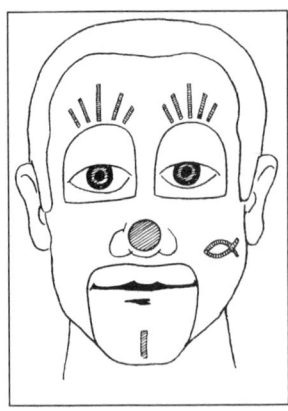 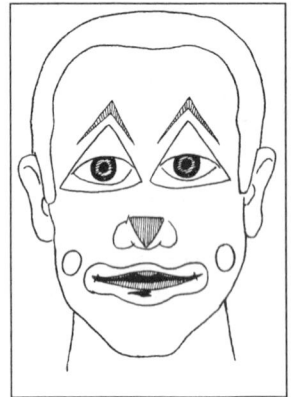 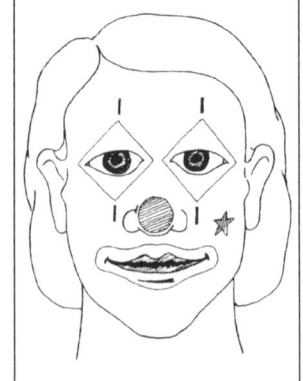 

Applying the Makeup

With a plan in place and supplies on hand, begin the process of applying makeup.

1. Clean the face thoroughly.
2. Apply a generous coating of cold cream.
3. With an eyeliner pencil, draw in the outlines of the eyes and mouth.
4. Apply Clown White to the eyes and mouth using either a makeup applicator or fingertips. Pat white areas gently with fingertips for a smooth and finished look.
5. Use the powder sock to pat the eyes and mouth thoroughly. (Use a generous amount of powder. This is the secret ingredient that keeps makeup from running and bubbling in hot weather and helps to set the makeup.)
6. Use the soft-bristled brush to remove excess powder from the face, being careful not to brush over the white makeup.
7. Set the makeup by misting the face with water.
8. Add color markings to the eyes and mouth and any special characters to the cheeks and nose.
9. Powder the colored areas lightly with a separate powder sock. (Use one sock for colors and one for white.)
10. Brush away excess powder from the face, if necessary, being careful not to brush over makeup.
11. Set the markings makeup by misting the face with water.
12. Check outlines of eyes and mouth, and redraw any that need enhancing.
13. Be sure the makeup includes a Christian symbol.

Remove makeup with tissues and vegetable oil or cold cream before washing the face with a washcloth. Once the greasepaint itself has been removed, wash the face with cleansing cream or mild soap and water. Clean makeup brushes and applicators by dipping them in vegetable oil, patting out makeup on a paper towel, and then soaking in warm water and a mild detergent.

Costumes

Equally important to the overall clown character is his or her costume. This fashion statement needs to be attractive, bright, comfortable, and easy to move around in. For a youth ministry, use homemade costumes or costumes pieced together with items from yard sales or thrift shops. Because of the more transient nature of youth in such a ministry, do not take on the expense of a professional costume as a full-time clown minister might.

Make costumes of lightweight material that does not wrinkle easily. Use bright colors and bold patterns. However, do not use materials featuring easily identifiable cartoon characters so as to avoid fictionalizing the message of the ministry. Several sewing patterns are available for various types of clown costumes, ranging from one- to two-piece outfits with ruffled collars to outfits of pants and vests.

Add some accessories to the costume for parades or one-on-one situations; however, such accessories might be a problem during clowning skits. For example, a large bead necklace might look cute on a clown during a parade, but it could easily be broken and spill beads for other clowns to slip on during a program. Hats are often added to costumes. Again, use these provided they will not be a hindrance or distraction.

God can use a clown's appearance to attract attention, but it is a clown's heart that God uses to reach out to a lost world.

Do not use earrings and other personal jewelry as part of a clown costume. Not only could these get in the way of clowning, but they could easily be lost or left behind in a dressing area. Do not use bright nail polish because this draws attention to the clown's hands rather than to the action being performed with those hands.

Oversized clown shoes are a natural laugh and may work well with adult or professional clowns. They are not, however, suggested for youth. Youth tend to be overzealous at times and may forget the cumbersome extra length on their feet, causing embarrassing falls. Canvas shoes (available in a number of colors) work best with youth because they are comfortable and provide good traction on most surfaces. Slick-bottomed shoes, sandals, or any type of slip-on shoes are strictly inappropriate.

These suggestions for makeup and costumes are just that—merely suggestions. Varying ministry situations, youth, and budgets all allow for a wide diversity of clowns. Regardless of their appearance, all Christian clowns share a common bond. Their task is to reveal Jesus Christ; and this cannot be accomplished with makeup and costumes alone. God can use a clown's appearance to attract attention, but it is a clown's heart that God uses to reach out to a lost world.

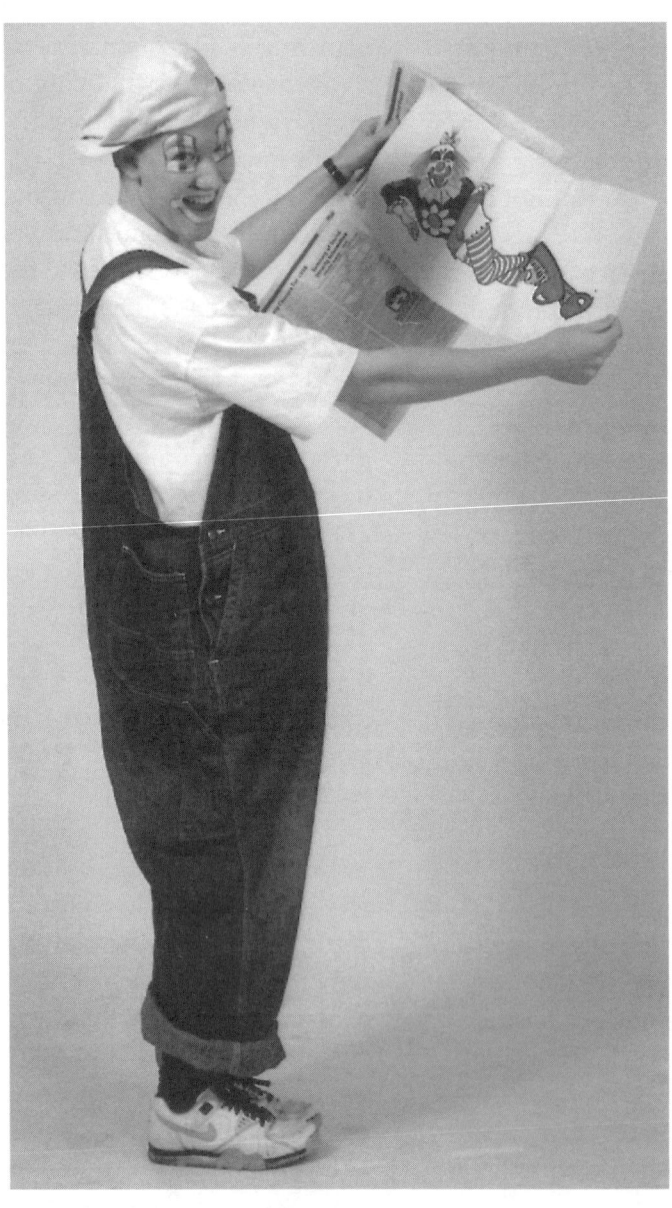

PLANNING FOR PROPS, SKITS, AND PROGRAMS

"Those who plan what is good find love and faithfulness" (Prov. 14:22 NIV).

Opportunities for clowning programs vary—from amusement parks to nursing homes, from the youngest of children to the oldest of senior adults—and these programs should be tailored to meet the needs of the specific target group. Build a repertoire of skits and program outlines that is flexible enough to interchange from time to time to meet these varying needs. This provides the adaptability necessary to keep the ministry in a state of readiness.

You should make two decisions early on regarding the type of clowning you will do. First, decide whether to talk or not to talk. Clowning skits are available with verbal exchange between clowns or between one clown and the audience; and others are available that use only pantomime action. As youth are usually hesitant to speak in front of large groups, and because public address systems may not always be accessible, pantomime skits are recommended for a youth clowning ministry.

Secondly, decide whether or not to use music during the skits. While it is not mandatory, the use of some type of music during skits helps to create a mood for the action and also helps youth feel less self-conscious. Use live music or audiotape and compact disc recordings. A favorite collection for background music includes the piano rags of Scott Joplin or calliope music. Unless the action of a skit is specifically designed to interpret the lyrics of a song, do not use music with words.

Staging Considerations

A clowning ministry is a mobile entity that encounters a large variety of staging areas. Clowns may find themselves in an established auditorium with orderly rows of seats. Or they may find themselves on a makeshift stage at the beach. They may even find themselves completely surrounded by curious onlookers in the middle of a park or schoolyard.

Execute all clowning action with a keen awareness of audience placement. Indoor situations may have a seating arrangement where all skit activity will play directly front and center. Or, the same seating arrangement may find only the right half of the room filled, requiring that you angle skit activity to the right to be effective. In outside situations, an audience may be fragmented in several different directions. Center all skits based on the location of the audience. If an audience is fragmented, begin front and center, and move the focus from side to side so that all members of the group are included in the action.

Props

Which comes first—the skits or the props? This is the proverbial chicken-or-the-egg situation. Secure props as skit needs arise, or purchase an interesting item spotted at a yard sale or toy store and wait for the right skit to come along. Professional props are available but are somewhat expensive. Try making props, when possible, or use household items already on hand for an inexpensive alternative.

Clown props that are either oversized or undersized draw attention and elicit an immediate audience reaction. For example, a clown would not use a small pocket comb to straighten a cowlick—he would use a 15-inch version. Similarly, a clown would not make a high-diving attempt into a large pool of water—he would plunge headlong into a drinking glass.

In addition to oversized or undersized objects, props may be ordinary, everyday objects that are used in ridiculous ways. For example, use a paint roller to apply soapy lather to a dog being bathed, or use a spoon to frantically transport water to douse a kitchen fire.

Some props are specifically designed for one particular skit. Others are used for numerous skits. By maintaining a storage closet for props and keeping a sharp eye out for prop possibilities, you can build a substantial storehouse of these tools of the trade in a relatively short period of time.

The Structure of Skits

The two most strategic and critical parts of any clowning skit are the beginning and the end—or the entrance and the exit. The entrance makes the initial contact with the audience and establishes a feeling of place, time, mood, and, in some cases, a situation. Audience contact and the creation of a particular setting are essential to the action that follows. If you do not communicate these elements clearly, the message of the skit may be lost. The exit brings all action to a conclusion, leaving the audience with the desired emotion or thought. A hurried exit, or one made before the audience is allowed to identify with the situation and empathize with the clown's emotions, may leave the audience confused.

In general, all skits follow a simple format:

1. **The Entrance or Opening.** This segment of a skit greets the audience and sets the place, mood, and sometimes a situation.

2. **The Exposition.** This segment reveals or clarifies the situation. If more than one clown is involved in the action, at least one other clown and possibly more arrive on the scene.

3. **The Conflict or Problem to Be Solved.** Interaction of clowns or the interaction of one clown with an object or situation results in some type of conflict. A problem arises that must be solved.

4. **The Solution.** Quite naturally, clowns do not solve a simple problem with a simple solution. They try a number of ridiculous means to resolve a conflict before the problem is either solved or the situation takes an unexpected and irreversible turn.

5. **The Exit.** All action is now completed and, with the desired emotion or thought firmly planted in the minds of audience members, the clowns depart. Exits can take the form of chase-offs or run-offs—in the case of comedy skits—or involve effects such as fade-outs when the concluding thought is a more serious one.

Types of Clowning Ministry Skits

Traditionally, secular clown skits are designed just for laughs or perhaps to create empathy for a particular clown character. Christian clowns use such comic skits to build a rapport with the audience. However, they use additional skits to provoke thought or reveal biblical truths. A complete clowning program may consist of a combination of comic, inspirational, and message skits.

A complete clowning program may consist of a combination of comic, inspirational, and message skits.

Comic skits are designed strictly for entertaining and attracting the attention of an audience. These reveal the clowns as bumbling but lovable characters involved in slapstick antics or silly pranks. As a general rule, the predicament is an ordinary one to which the clowns react with several ridiculous solutions, usually ending in calamity and a run-off or chase-off ending.

Inspirational skits are those designed to depict some type of moral value. The clowns are involved in a situation in which they have to make a decision between right and wrong. While still quite comical and using the traditional ridiculous attempts, these skits ultimately resolve the problem in a manner consistent with biblical values, and the concluding thought is a lesson learned.

Message skits are those designed to reveal a specific biblical truth. The clowns are involved in situations in which a behavior needs to be changed. After several unsuccessful attempts with worldly solutions, the clown comes to the realization that Jesus Christ is the solution. Endings for message skits are often fade-outs that leave the audience with time to reflect on their own life situations and to identify with and accept the clown's revelation.

Matching Skits with Age Groups

Some skits (comic routines in particular) are appropriate for and enjoyed equally by any age group. Others may meet the needs of one age group in particular. Knowing how to plan a program of skits that meets the needs of a specific target or age group enhances the effectiveness of a clowning ministry. An adult audience may lose interest long before a message can be given if the opening skits are too simple or trite. Likewise, skits too complicated or symbolic for children may cause them to become distracted.

If you know the age of an audience in advance, plan a program that addresses the needs of that particular age group. If not, or if the audience will include a wide range of ages, plan a program of skits that vary in length and content. It is always best to keep the message simple and aimed at the youngest members of a potential audience. Although teenagers and adults may not find such a simple message as thought-provoking, they will still clearly understand it.

Consider the following factors when matching skits to specific age groups.

1. Children (as well as mentally challenged adults) have a great deal of imagination. They do not require elaborate detail within a clowning skit, as they can enter the clown's world of fantasy quite easily. Children seem to enjoy and respond best to slapstick comedy in comic skits, to simple story lines in inspirational skits centered around situations with which they can personally identify, and to very basic Bible truths in message skits.

2. Youth are imaginative, but at the same time have become skeptical of the clown's world of fantasy. While they can eventually become a part of this world, it takes them a little longer to do so than a child. Skits for youth should contain more detailed information about the action. Comic skits of any type

appeal to this audience, and they respond well to inspirational skits that involve age-appropriate situations (such as peer pressure, self-esteem and acceptance, or friendship) and to message skits that relate Bible truths to life problems with which they can personally identify (such as frustration, broken relationships or promises, or choosing right from wrong).

3. Adults readily distinguish things imagined from reality. Because of this it is more difficult to draw them into the clown's world of fantasy. To become a part of that fantasy, they must relinquish a certain amount of personal control and are generally reluctant to do so. As a result, adults tend to perceive the action from a distance and not as a participant in the clown's world. Comic skits of any type appeal to adults. They respond well to inspirational skits that portray solutions for conflict in relationships (parent-child, husband-wife, friend-friend) and to message skits that relate Bible truths to daily problems they may face (making wise choices, living a Christian life in a secular world, or handling disappointment or grief). They also respond well to truths that may cause them to evaluate their own spiritual condition.

4. Senior adults too tend to perceive clowns from a distance, although they are more likely to relinquish their reality control than are younger adults. Any comic skit will bring joy and laughter. Inspirational skits that reinforce their moral values and message skits that provide reassurance of God's love and mercy are particularly meaningful to them at this stage of their life. Because a senior adult may be more concerned with death and eternal life, the simple message of salvation will not only assure those who have already received Jesus Christ as their Savior but will also provide direction for those who still seek Him.

Outlining a Basic Clowning Program

A clowning program is made up of several short skits or one long skit (30 to 45 minutes). Longer skits are suitable for older audiences in controlled settings; shorter skits are suitable for mixed-age audiences or for resort or outside situations. Based on the premise that a youth ministry is more likely to be involved with the latter, the following outline has proven effective.

Introduction. At the outset of any program, the narrator (a modern version of the more traditional ringmaster) makes any necessary introductory comments, such as announcing the name of the ministry, the church it represents, and what it hopes to accomplish through the program. This introductory time can also be used as a lead-in to the clowning program itself, with several of the clowns playing tricks on the narrator for a few laughs.

Comic Skits. Begin any clowning program, particularly when the audience may contain unchurched persons, with a few comic skits—skits designed just for laughs. These skits grab the attention of an audience and begin to build a relationship that will encourage them to stay for the remainder of a program. Comic skits are especially useful in resort or park settings where an audience may continue gathering even after a program has begun.

Inspirational Skits. Following the comic skits, present one or two inspirational skits. These routines usually teach a moral lesson; and although the action is still comical, the theme content enables the audience to make the transition from slapstick humor to a more serious mood.

Message Skits. The last two or three routines of a program may include message skits—those having a biblical message or truth. These will differ with the theme of each program and the age of an audience. However, the purpose remains the same: to show the world's predicament of sin and to offer Jesus Christ as the solution.

Conclusion. The conclusion of a clowning program depends on the interests and talents of the youth in a particular ministry. Some groups learn sign language and use it to interpret a contemporary worship song. Others simply pantomime a worship song as a closing skit. Still others read a Scripture verse and share a devotional thought or a prayer. Whatever the choice, closing each program with a time of worship allows an audience to absorb the message and evaluate their own spiritual condition, thus opening doors for witnessing opportunities.

One-on-One Time. Plan some type of one-on-one activity to follow each clowning program. The skits already presented provide a natural stimulus for children and even adults to ask questions or make comments. Activities with small children might include prizes, games, face painting, or balloon sculpturing. During the conversation with the child, clowns can reinforce the Bible truths portrayed earlier. With youth or adults, one-on-one activities may include age-appropriate giveaways, refreshments, or fellowship-building games. With senior adults, particularly those in a nursing care facility, one-on-one activities could include favors, instant camera pictures taken with clowns, or simply a time of personal conversation.

These programming ideas have proven to be effective with youth clowning ministries. Use them as a starting point for your own ideas. It is important to plan and to organize, then follow God's leading. Sound planning eliminates many potential headaches and embarrassments. However, each member of a clowning ministry must remain alert to see how God is working around and through him or her. When a door opens for witnessing, even the best-laid plans need to be flexible enough to be changed in order to meet the needs at hand.

7

Ministry Ideas

"As the Father has sent me, I am sending you" (John 20:21 NIV).

Ministry opportunities for a clowning troupe are as diverse as the individual clowns themselves. Just as there are few places where joy and laughter are not appropriate or appreciated, there are few places where clowns are not welcomed. The greatest gift we have to offer is the joy of God's love, and that is needed in any setting.

The key to a dynamic clowning ministry is adaptability. Some opportunities may call for a program of skits lasting anywhere from 15 to 45 minutes or more. Other opportunities may call simply for one-on-one contact. A ministry flexible enough to adjust to changing situations will be effective in reaching out to the needs of others.

Once a clowning troupe has been out in the community and gained some exposure, word-of-mouth promotion may keep the group busy for months. At other times, it may be necessary to seek out opportunities in the community. Here are a few to try.

Churches

Begin by exploring opportunities within your own church or within other churches in your community. Use clowning for special emphasis programs such as promoting particular offerings or events, family night suppers, enlistment events for Vacation Bible Schools, or holiday programs.

A home audience is warm and loving and provides an excellent first experience for new clowns who are hesitant about being accepted. A positive initial clowning experience helps new clowns gain confidence in their skills as well as their ability to witness. In addition, even a home church audience has people who need to be comforted by a good dose of laughter or a message of hope.

Missions Activities

If your church or youth program sponsors missions activities throughout the year, plan ways to use the clowning ministry as part of those projects. Clowns can provide short skits, face painting, or balloons at a missions fair. They can distribute flyers and promote a neighborhood Bible club. They are a valuable asset to a youth missions team because they provide both programs and witnessing skills.

Nursing Homes

Elderly people, particularly those requiring nursing care, are especially open to the gospel and the comfort of the Scriptures. Having lost their mobility, and in some cases even their means of communication, they feel isolated and alone. Clowns can bring smiles to lonely faces.

Opportunities may allow for a full program of skits if residents are able to gather in a dining hall or recreation area. Even those who have trouble seeing will enjoy the lively music and laughter that fills the room.

Follow the program with a one-on-one time. Clowns can serve refreshments or simply talk with the residents. An instant picture camera is a good investment. Clowns can take photographs with residents, then sign them with a simple, "Jesus loves you . . . and so do I!" as a keepsake of the day for the residents' bulletin board. However, before taking any photographs, check with the administrator about regulations. In some instances this may be prohibited without written consent of a family or staff member.

Follow the program with room-to-room visitation (if allowed) to those residents who were not able to move to the program area. Just the presence of a clown can cheer a resident. Clowns can talk and leave a small favor or devotional book . . . but this is no place for balloons that can pop!

Mentally Disabled Adults/Children

Most communities have group homes for mentally disabled adults and children, or centers where these adults gather from time to time. This audience is usually eager to be a part of the action and will respond with loud laughter and applause—a most appreciative audience and one that will be a good experience for new clowns provided they are trained to respond to mentally disabled people.

Plan for some type of one-on-one activity following a program with this group, as some will want to be close to the clowns who have brought them such happiness. Distribute prizes or take instant picture camera photographs to leave with the adults.

If a Special Olympics event is held in your community, a clowning ministry can participate with walk-around gags, balloons, and prizes. Clowns can even serve as official race starters or as personal encouragers for participants.

Afterschool Care Programs

While public schools may not welcome a Christ-centered clowning program for the school at large, many afterschool care programs sponsored by churches, YMCAs, or other organizations do. Tailor a program for such a group to meet the requirements of the school, if necessary. This is not to fault the school itself as it must meet certain regulations regarding religious activities. Take this into consideration when planning programs.

Here, face painting and balloon sculpturing fit well, as both allow plenty of time to talk with the children individually. A good conversational witness goes a long way!

Afterschool care centers look for holiday programs, and some have monthly birthday parties in which a clowning ministry can participate.

Children's Hospitals

Unless a hospital is equipped with a dayroom where you can present a clowning program to children, it is unlikely that you can provide a program of skits in this situation. Instead, consider room-to-room visitation to deliver smiles and small gifts such as coloring books and crayons, reading books, puzzles, and other items that a bedridden child can use. Some special considerations for this ministry include:

- Avoid balloons that can pop.
- Take care not to make a lot of noise.
- Do not include candy or sweets as prizes.

- Be sensitive to the medical and emotional condition of each child.
- Be certain the clowns are trained to face any medical conditions they may see in such an environment.

Community Events/Parades

Community events often lend themselves to an opportunity for a clowning ministry. Here again, do not overstep boundaries when dealing with religious restrictions. Annual Fourth of July celebrations, craft fairs, store openings, malls, parks, and other such events all provide opportunities for clowning. If you are not already familiar with annual community events, watch the local newspaper. Keep a file of such festivities and contact the appropriate officials in time for the next event.

While parades offer an opportunity for exposure of a clowning ministry to the community, they do not offer the best witnessing opportunities. However, a float or even a walking entry with a prominent sign promoting the group will make the community aware of the ministry and can result in other opportunities later. Check with parade officials to see if tracts, Bible verse stickers, or other similar prizes can be given out by walking clowns.

Senior Citizens Groups

Virtually every community has senior citizens groups and other civic organizations. Senior centers, young-at-heart clubs, meal sites, church groups, and other senior organizations are constantly looking for programs for their meetings. These groups are more likely to be open to a religious message, and a program of skits often works well. You may also use clowns for a simple sing-along (complete with clowning antics, of course!) or just a surprise visit during a luncheon to distribute favors or prizes.

Parties for Disadvantaged Children

Several community agencies sponsor holiday parties or other activities for disadvantaged children, the families of prisoners, and other groups. Contact appropriate agencies and plan a time to present a clowning program for these groups. If possible, work with other missions or youth groups within your church to sponsor such a party. Follow the program with face painting or balloon sculpturing for a one-on-one contact with the children.

Malls, Parks, YMCAs, etc.

Check with managers or directors for guidelines and/or restrictions in these areas. Shopping malls, parks, or YMCAs—particularly in conjunction with a community event such as a craft fair, membership drive, or carnival—provide a number of opportunities for a clowning ministry. While a formal program of skits may not be appropriate in these locations, walk-around gags, balloon sculpturing, or a face-painting booth can draw attention and provide times for personal contact.

There is indeed an abundance of opportunities for a clowning ministry in any community! The need for laughter and hope is great and brings a welcomed change from the day-to-day problems of the world. May God richly bless you and the youth you lead as you reach out in His name and for His glory.

Appendix A
Sample Skits

Note: All skits are original by the author except where adaptations and collaborations are noted. In all skits in this section the words *he*, *his*, and *him* are intended to also refer to *she*, *hers*, and *her*.

This appendix contains a sampling of skits that can be used in a clowning program for unchurched persons and includes routines for children, youth, and adults.

Adapting Skits for Use

Among the skit offerings of this or any other clowning book some routines may appear impractical due to the number of clowns needed, special props required, timing, or content. Indeed, a ministry cannot use every skit. Some need to be presented strictly as written. However, with a little imagination, many are adaptable to fit a variety of ministry circumstances.

Study the routines carefully and ask questions. Are all the roles essential to the message or thought of the skit? Can one clown play more than one role? Can we add one or more roles without confusing the message of the skit? What props can we substitute for items that are not available? Can we alter a skit containing dialogue with one using pantomime? What actions are essential to the message, and which can we eliminate to shorten the skit?

Adapt skits for the size of a particular ministry. Not all clowns in a ministry will be involved in every skit. However, involve each clown in at least three or four routines so that his or her character can build a relationship with the audience. Naturally, individual clowns involved with a smaller ministry will participate in a greater number of skits than will the clowns in a larger ministry.

If a ministry has a small number of clowns (2 to 4 members, for example), they need not disregard all skits that require 5 or more clowns. Often, a routine contains several small parts in which clowns make a brief appearance to complete only one specific action and then depart. A smaller ministry can use such a skit by assigning two or more minor roles to the same clown; or perhaps by eliminating one of the lesser roles entirely without affecting the meaning of the skit.

If a clowning ministry is rather large (8 to 12 members or more), do not overlook skits written for 1 to 4 clowns. Watch for a series of lesser roles written to be played by 1 clown and use more than 1 clown to fill these roles. You can add a new character or situation without confusing the thought or message.

Adapt the length of skits to fit specific needs. The clowns themselves can control the length of most pantomime skits. When you need shorter skits, study routines to determine the most essential actions and concentrate only on these. Add length by allowing clowns more time for audience takes or for expressing emotions. Add slapstick humor to accentuate an action, or just to get a laugh! Before you adjust a skit for timing, try it in front of an audience. Youth tend to move through clowning actions much faster during a program than during rehearsals!

Adapt skits to available props. Do not toss skits aside because a special piece of equipment or a particular prop is unavailable. Use handmade props to replace more elaborate items, and use alternate methods of achieving a special effect if a piece of equipment is not available. Occasionally, you can use props on hand as substitutes in skits.

This appendix contains the following skit outlines.

Comic Skits

The Statue (all ages). A statue comes to life and shows that things are not always what they appear.

Portrait Perils (all ages). An unsuspecting customer gets a surprise portrait from a painter who takes a little too much artistic license.

Washday (all ages). An ordinary task turns into frustration and disaster with the help of an animated clothesline!

The Hypnotist (all ages). The tables are turned on a performing hypnotist when one of his volunteers remains in a trance.

Inspirational Skits

The Choir (children; includes adaptations for youth and adults). Realizing that practice makes perfect, a clown learns to strive to do his best. Based on 2 Timothy 2:15: "Do your best to present yourself to God as one approved."

Color-Blind (children; includes adaptations for youth and adults). Two clowns overcome prejudice to show love for one another. Based on 1 John 4:11: "Dear friends, since God so loved us, we also ought to love one another."

It Ain't Heavy . . . I Have a Brother (youth; includes adaptations for children and adults). A clown offers to share another's burden as they handle some heavy problems for the Cares and Woe Packing Company. Based on Galatians 6:2: "Carry each other's burdens, and in this way you will fulfill the law of Christ."

Message Skits

Ooey-Gooey (youth and adults). A curious clown ends up in a very sticky situation. Two helpful wallpaper hangers show him that God will forgive us when we confess our sins. Based on 1 John 1:9: "If we confess our sins, he is faithful and just and will forgive us our sins and purify us from all unrighteousness."

The Pesky Fly (youth and adults; includes adaptation for older children). A fly that has been annoying two clowns is finally caught. The clowns have trouble deciding what to do with the pest until one of the clown demonstrates God's mercy. Based on 1 Peter 1:3: "In his great mercy he has given us new birth into a living hope through the resurrection of Jesus Christ from the dead."

Which Way? (youth and adults). After a frustrating traveling experience on Wide Road, a clown learns that the only way to salvation and eternal life is through Jesus Christ. Based on John 14:6: "Jesus answered, 'I am the way—and the truth and the life. No one comes to the Father except through me.'"

THE STATUE

(Based on an anonymous, classic clown gag.)

TYPE OF SKIT: Comic

TARGET AUDIENCE: All ages

LENGTH OF SKIT: Two to five minutes

CAST OF CLOWNS: The Boss
The Worker
The Statue

PROPS NEEDED: Chair
Comics
Large feather duster
Help Wanted Sign
(See Prop Notes
following skit outline.)

SETUP: Scene opens with the Statue striking a pose off to one side and the Boss sitting in the chair, either reading the comics or taking a nap. Place the Help Wanted sign in full view of the audience (either propped against the Statue or the Boss's chair).

The Boss sits idly in his chair reading the daily funnies (or perhaps catching 40 winks!). Off to one side stands the Statue, striking a pose and not moving a muscle. The Worker enters the scene and acknowledges the audience, stopping when he sees the Help Wanted sign. He points the sign out to the audience and indicates his interest in the position. Convinced that he is the right man for the job, the Worker straightens his clothes, slicks back his hair, improves his posture, takes the Help Wanted sign in hand, and approaches the Boss. He taps the Boss on the shoulder to get his attention. No response. He pushes the Boss's shoulder. Still no response. He pushes a little harder this time, and at last the Boss notices him!

The Boss is somewhat irritated at being disturbed from his reading (napping), but as the Worker displays the Help Wanted sign and indicates that he would like the job, the Boss's attitude changes to one of delight. At last! Someone to do the dirty work! The Boss picks up the feather duster and hands it to the Worker. Leading the Worker over toward the Statue, the Boss indicates that the job entails dusting the Statue. Simple, right? The Worker assures the Boss that he understands. "OK, I've got it." Satisfied that the job is in good hands, the Boss returns to his chair.

The Worker begins dusting the Statue. Hey, this seems easy enough. As the Worker moves toward the back, the Statue breaks into a large smile and winks at the audience, letting them know that he is no ordinary statue! The Worker moves back around toward the front of the Statue, who quickly regains his statuesque expression. As the Worker bends over in front of the Statue to dust the feet, the Statue taps him on the shoulder. The Worker slowly turns to look first at the audience and then straightens to look at the Statue. The Statue gives a large smile and wink to the Worker.

Upon seeing the Statue come to life, the Worker jumps up in fright, screams, and runs back to the Boss in a panic. As the Worker is returning to the Boss, the Statue does a large belly laugh, points mockingly at the running Worker, and then snaps back into position—but in a different pose this time.

The Worker shakes the Boss from his reading (or nap) and excitedly tries to explain what has just transpired with the Statue. Naturally, the Boss cannot believe what he is hearing.

This Worker must be completely loony! Statues don't move—they're made of stone, for goodness sake! The Boss sternly indicates that the Worker must be seeing things and insists that he return to his cleaning.

Apprehensively, the Worker returns to the Statue, indicating his nervousness to the audience. Hey, wait a minute! What's this? As he nears the Statue, he notices that something is different. He models the first pose he remembers and then the new one the Statue has now assumed. Cautiously, the Worker takes a few quick swipes at the Statue with the duster. The Statue doesn't move. "Oh, well," the Worker thinks. "It must have been my imagination." And he begins dusting the Statue once again.

Again, as the Worker moves to the back, the Statue smiles and winks at the audience. As the Worker comes back around to the front of the Statue and bends down to dust the feet, the Statue taps him on the shoulder. The Worker turns his head toward the audience to indicate, "Oh, no! Not again!" Then ever so slowly, with the feather duster shaking slightly in his hand, the Worker stands and looks at the Statue, who promptly places a hand beneath his chin, wiggles his fingers, and sticks out his tongue.

The Worker again jumps up in fright, screams, and runs back to the Boss to tell his tale. As the Worker is returning to the Boss, the Statue does a large belly laugh, points at the running Worker, and then snaps back into position—but in a third different pose.

The Worker shakes the Boss and frantically tries to explain the latest development. He emphatically returns the feather duster to the Boss. No way is he going to continue with this job! As the Worker starts to leave, the Boss jumps up and drags him back. *(This can be either a pulling action or a pushing action as the Boss grabs the* Worker, *then gets behind him to push him back toward the Statue. The Worker will naturally resist, but eventually will end up in front of the Statue.)*

This time the Boss returns to the Statue with the Worker to show him that nothing is unusual and that the Worker must be losing his mind.

The Boss instructs the Worker to begin dusting. The feather duster is shaking uncontrollably in the Worker's hand, and as he reaches out with the other arm to steady it, both arms begin shaking. The shaking eventually works its way to the Worker's legs until his whole body is shaking in fear. The Boss grabs the Worker and steadies him. Then he points to the Statue's shoulder and the Worker gives it a quick dusting. While the Boss and the Worker move to the back, the dusting continues. Meanwhile, the Statue again gives his smile and wink to the audience.

The Boss and the Worker make their way back around to the front of the Statue and the Boss points to the Statue's feet. Both the Boss and the Worker bend over in front of the Statue *(The Boss and the Worker should face one another.)*. As they do, the Statue taps both of them on the back. The Boss and the Worker look at each other, then toward the audience, and then slowly up to the Statue *(actions should be synchronized)*. They look up to find the Statue smiling down at them. As the Statue waves and shouts *"Boo!"* both the Boss and the Worker jump up, scream, and run off stage. The Statue exits, laughing raucously at the two bumbling clowns!

Prop Notes: If you cannot find a large feather duster, purchase two or three smaller, less expensive, and perhaps more colorful ones and bind them together with clear mailing tape. Make the Help Wanted sign from poster board (about 10-by-14 inches) with string attached for hanging the sign on a chair or the arm of the Statue. A laminated sign or one coated with clear adhesive covering will prevent damage and will store well. Some type of small table for the Boss to prop his feet on is an optional item for this skit. If you use the table, the Help Wanted sign might then dangle from the Boss's feet at the beginning of the skit.

PORTRAIT PERILS

(Based on an anonymous, classic clown gag.)

TYPE OF SKIT: Comic

TARGET AUDIENCE: All ages

LENGTH OF SKIT: Four to seven minutes

CAST OF CLOWNS: The Artist
　　　　　　　　　The Assistant
　　　　　　　　　The Subject

PROPS NEEDED: Chair
　　　　　　　Small table (or easel stand)
　　　　　　　Large crayons (or oversized paintbrush and palate)
　　　　　　　Oversized comb
　　　　　　　Handheld mirror
　　　　　　　Easel board with picture of donkey (or monkey, etc.)
　　　　　　　Sign: Portraits—$100
　　　　　　　Oversized folding money
　　　　　　　(See Prop Notes following skit outline.)

SETUP: Set small table (or easel stand) a little to one side of center stage. Place the easel board with the picture of the donkey on the table or easel so that the audience cannot see the Portrait. Place the Portraits—$100 sign near the easel and the chair to the other side of center stage. Place the mirror and comb under the chair or have the Assistant bring them in as he enters.

The Artist and the Assistant enter as the Artist takes several exaggerated bows to the audience and the Assistant bumbles in carrying the oversized crayons and dropping them clumsily several times. While the Assistant expresses apologies, the Artist expresses irritation. The Assistant goes about the business of arranging the crayons, putting out the Portraits—$100 sign, and dusting off the chair to prepare for the first customer. The Artist, meanwhile, stands near the easel stretching and flexing his fingers to prepare for his masterpiece.

About this time, the Subject arrives on the scene and the Assistant hurries out to grab him. The Assistant points to the sign as the Artist sizes up the Subject and indicates that his face is perfect for a beautiful portrait. The Subject, vain as he is, must agree with the Artist and hands over the money. Well, it's not *all* the money. The Artist eagerly counts the bills and realizes there are a few missing. He taps his foot and holds out his hand impatiently for the rest, which the Subject reluctantly gives him. The Artist double-checks the amount, then the Assistant shows the Subject to the chair.

Again, the Artist begins flexing and stretching and imagining his subject on canvas while the Assistant is busy posing the Subject in the chair. *(The Assistant places the Subject's hand on top of his head, crosses his legs, or otherwise poses him into an odd position.)* The Assistant gives the Subject a quick hair combing and then only a brief glance in the mirror before indicating to the Artist that he is ready. The Artist selects a crayon (or maybe even one for each hand!) and frantically begins sketching as the Assistant excitedly looks on.

About this time, the Subject releases his pose and waves to the audience as if he has just noticed them for the first time. The irritated Artist stops his work, stomps his foot, and calls the Subject's behavior to the attention of the

Assistant. The Assistant scolds the Subject and resets the pose, and gives another even quicker hair combing and an even more brief glance in the mirror before indicating to the Artist that he can begin once again. The Artist gets in only a few strokes before the Subject again drops his pose and begins waving to the audience. Now the Artist is really getting angry and again indicates to the Assistant that the Subject needs reposing. For the second time, the Assistant returns to the Subject and repeats the business of posing him. "Now hold still!" the Assistant warns the Subject before telling the Artist that he can resume his work.

The Artist begins drawing, and the Subject again drops his pose and begins waving and smiling to the audience. The Artist has just about had all he is going to take and indicates the Subject's unruly behavior to the Assistant. The Assistant does a slow turn of the head, moving his gaze from the Artist to the Subject and then back to the Artist. The Artist simply points sternly to the Subject; and the Assistant sighs, pushes up his sleeves in determination, and returns to scold the Subject yet again. Upon seeing the Assistant approaching in such a manner, the Subject snaps back into the correct pose himself! "That's more like it," the Assistant thinks, and returns to watch the Artist work.

After few more strokes of the crayon, the Artist has at long last completed his work. He wipes the perspiration from his forehead and asks the Assistant to take a peek. The Assistant indicates to the Artist and then to the audience that it is indeed a magnificent piece of art. The Subject drops his pose and gets ready to see the masterpiece.

The Artist must agree that this is indeed his finest work! He picks up the easel board, being careful not to reveal it to the Subject, and begins showing the portrait to the audience first, working his way around in a semicircular fashion so that the Subject is the last to see the finished product. Naturally, when the Subject does finally see the portrait, he is outraged, jumps up, and begins chasing the Artist. They circle the stage and then exit with the Assistant running after them both!

Prop Notes: Use a small table (approximately 18 to 24 inches high) to support a self-standing easel board. Or, if an actual easel stand is available, prop the Artist's painting there. (Of the two, the small table has more mobility and requires less assembly at the program site.)

Purchase the large crayons through specialty clowning shops or purchase them ready-made in card shops as rolls of wrapping paper with plastic crayon tips. You can also make crayons by painting cardboard inserts from large rolls of wrapping paper and using hot glue to attach either a plastic foam or cardboard tip. Should you choose to use paintbrush and palate, purchase them from a specialty shop; or form the brush from papier mâché with bristles (doll's hair from a craft shop) attached. Make the palate from thick cardboard with appropriate colors painted on.

You can purchase the oversized comb and handheld mirror inexpensively from any department store. Make oversized folding money on a copier by using the enlargement feature and printing play money onto green paper. Cut the bills to a uniform size. Make the Portraits—$100 sign at least 10 inches by 14 inches in size. A laminated sign or one coated with clear adhesive covering will withstand repeated use and prolonged storage.

Make a self-supporting easel board by attaching two poster-sized pieces of thick cardboard at one end with clear mailing tape. Attach a length (about 8 to 10 inches) of wide black grosgrain ribbon to connect the two cardboard pieces on each side. Draw a picture of a cartoon-type donkey, monkey, or other comical creature on a large piece of white poster board and attach it to the easel. If possible, laminate the poster or coat it with clear adhesive covering to avoid damage.

WASHDAY

TYPE OF SKIT: Comic

TARGET AUDIENCE: All ages

LENGTH OF SKIT: Two to four minutes

CAST OF CLOWNS: The Washer
                      Two Lineholders

PROPS NEEDED: Chair
                Large tub
                Clown suit or large clown boxer shorts
                Clothesline (approximately 8 to 10 feet long)
                Clothespins
                Box marked *Soap*
                (See Prop Notes following skit outline.)

SETUP: The two Lineholders stand on the stage area off to one side with sufficient space for the Washer to move to the back side of the line. Set the chair with tub directly in front at center stage with a few clothespins on the floor beside the tub.

The Washer enters and acknowledges the audience with a wave and by showing them his dirty clown suit (or boxer shorts). Phew! Not only is it dirty, but it smells pretty bad, too! The Washer takes his place in the chair, pours in a little soap, and begins scrubbing his clothes the old fashioned way. Boy, this is hard work! He wipes the perspiration from his forehead. At last, the clothes seem to be clean and he wrings out the excess water (imaginary, of course!). He stands, shakes out the clothes, and moves to the back side of the clothesline (so that the Washer is facing the audience). Just as the Washer is putting the clothes over the line, the Lineholders move the clothesline suddenly downward—much to the surprise of the Washer. The Washer tries to adjust, and bends over to put his clothes on the lowered line *(being extremely careful not to put his own face over the line to avoid injury in the next move!)*. Just as the Washer is about to reach the line, the Lineholders suddenly move the clothesline upward high over the Washer's head. *(Care must be taken here to avoid injury to the Washer!)* The Washer grabs the line and pulls it down to the correct height, gives each Lineholder a stern look, and is at last able to place his clothes over the line. Oh, no! The Washer begins feeling around in his pockets. Unbelievable! He forgot the clothespins. The Washer points to the clothespins still laying beside the washtub. Leaving his clothes draped across the line, the Washer returns to the tub for the clothespins.

As he does so (and while he is not looking), the Lineholders wiggle the line until the clothes fall to the ground. the Washer collects the clothespins and turns back to the line. "What's this?" His clean clothes are on the ground! Somewhat irritated, the Washer picks the clothes up and returns to the tub. There is nothing to do but begin again. He adds a little more soap to the water and begins scrubbing all over again—not too happy about the situation! Once the clothes are clean, he wrings out the excess water and returns to the back side of the line.

The Washer is skeptical about these Lineholders now and cautiously starts to place the clothes over the line. One of the Lineholders quickly moves his end of the line up high while at the same time the other Lineholder

45

moves his end to the ground, causing a sharp diagonal. The Washer moves to the higher end of the line and starts to place the clothes on it. But, before the clothes can touch the line, the Lineholders quickly switch the diagonal with the higher end going to the ground and the ground level end moving up high. "This is getting exasperating!" thinks the Washer, and moves to the higher end once again. This time he is able to place the clothes on the line, but they slide down the diagonal. The Washer catches the clothes just before they hit the ground. He then moves to each Lineholder and brings both ends of the line to the right position, scolding the Lineholders so they will hold still. Then he carefully lays his clothes over the line. Oh, no! Not again! The Washer points to the clothespins beside the washtub that he has forgotten for the second time!

As the Washer returns for the clothespins, the Lineholders once again wiggle the line causing the clothes to fall to the ground. The Washer turns to find his clothes in the dirt once more and is enraged! He snaps up the clothes, slams them back into the washtub, empties the box of soap into the tub, and furiously begins scrubbing. When the clothes are clean, he squeezes the excess water out, using full force and venting his anger in the process.

Aha! The Washer has an idea! He will not be caught without his clothespins *this* time! The Washer picks up several clothespins, displays them to the audience and then cleverly attaches them to his sleeve. He moves to the back of the clothesline and warns the Lineholders not to move. The Washer grabs the line dead center, and although the Lineholders try more tricks, they are to no avail and the line is held still. The Washer places the clothes on the line and attaches the clothespins. Victory at last!

The Washer walks away from the line, brushing his hands together in smug satisfaction. After a few steps *(and when the Washer is positioned in front of the line)*, the Washer stops. His expression changes from satisfaction to building disappointment. He looks at the audience and then into the sky. He holds out a hand to feel the raindrops, indicates the changing weather condition to the audience, and begins sobbing. As the rain comes down even harder, the Washer grabs his clothes still attached to the line and, followed by the Lineholders, runs off stage.

Prop Notes: You can use an authentic metal washtub for this skit; however, a larger, brightly colored plastic one purchased from a department store will serve not only as a washtub but can also be used to carry and store props! The clothes to be washed should be made of durable material to withstand repeated wringing. A clown suit is funny; a pair of oversized clown boxer shorts is even funnier and can easily be made using bright printed fabric. Use thick clothesline rather than ordinary packing string for this skit, as the latter will not withstand the weight of the clothes or the tugging and pulling antics of the Lineholders. Use inexpensive, plastic spring-type clothespins, and create the box of soap by covering an empty detergent box with white paper and printing the word *Soap* on both the front and the back.

THE HYPNOTIST

(Adapted for four clowns and based on the "chase-off" scene in a similar skit by Happy Jack Feder.)

TYPE OF SKIT: Comic

TARGET AUDIENCE: All ages

LENGTH OF SKIT: Three to five minutes

CAST OF CLOWNS: The Hypnotist
        Victim 1
        Victim 2
        Victim 3

PROPS NEEDED: Chair
        Magic wand
        Bell
        Large whistle
        Foam bat
        (See Prop Notes following skit outline.)

SETUP: Set the chair center stage and hide the foam bat behind it. Place the magic wand, bell, and whistle beside the chair.

The Hypnotist enters rather pompously and makes a large bow to the audience, encouraging their applause. After a quick dusting of the chair and an arranging of the bell and whistle, the Hypnotist picks up his magic wand and shows it to the audience. He indicates what is about to transpire by circling the wand in front of his own face and pretending to fall asleep.

Now, the Hypnotist is ready for volunteers! He places his hand above his eyes and begins searching for the right person. (*All other clowns in the group will take part in the audience; however, the Victims will have been determined beforehand.*

As the Hypnotist is searching for a volunteer, all clowns will begin waving their arms and begging to be selected.) Victim 1 is chosen and excitedly comes to the stage, taking a seat. He is thrilled at the prospect of being hypnotized and cannot wait to begin.

With pantomime action, the Hypnotist indicates both to Victim 1 and to the audience that he will circle the wand in front of the face of Victim 1 causing him to fall asleep. Oh, boy! Victim 1 thinks that's a great idea! The Hypnotist asks for absolute quiet from the audience. Then he slowly begins circling the wand as Victim 1 follows the movement with his eyes. After several circles, Victim 1 begins to get drowsy—his head starts to wobble a little and his eyes begin rolling back in his head. At last, Victim 1's head bobs forward and he is asleep.

The Hypnotist picks up the bell and the whistle. Hmmm. He strokes his chin in deep thought and finally gets an idea! He has decided to have Victim 1 do some jumping jacks. He indicates to the audience that when he rings the bell, the action will begin, and when he blows the whistle, the action will stop, and that Victim 1 won't remember a thing. Again, the Hypnotist asks for complete silence. Holding the bell close to the ear of Victim 1, the Hypnotist gives it a loud ring. Victim 1, in a trancelike state, springs out of the chair and begins doing jumping jacks. (*Members of the clown audience lead in applause for the feat.*) After several seconds of the action, the Hypnotist blows the whistle. Victim 1 immediately stops and, realizing that he has probably made a fool of himself, he slinks back to his place in the audience.

Now, it's time for Victim 2. Again, the Hypnotist searches the audience and all clowns wave their arms in the air to be selected. Victim 2 is chosen and very nervously approaches the stage to sit in the chair. As he sits down, his fingers lock around the edges of the chair in a tight grip. The Hypnotist asks for silence and starts to circle the wand in front of Victim 2's face. Before a full circle has been completed, Victim 2 goes completely limp and slides out of the chair. "What's this?" the Hypnotist thinks. No one has ever gone under that quickly. He waves a hand in front of Victim 2's face. No response. He pinches Victim 2. Still no response. Oh, well, he must really be asleep. Now, what to do with Victim 2. The Hypnotist has an idea! He indicates to the audience that he will cause Victim 2 to imitate a chicken. He picks up the bell and rings it in Victim 2's ear. Immediately Victim 2 jumps to his feet and begins clucking loudly and walking around like a chicken. *(Members of the clown audience lead in applause for the feat.)* After several seconds of the action, the Hypnotist blows the whistle and Victim 2 immediately stops. Realizing that he, too, has probably made a fool of himself, he shyly returns to his place in the audience.

Time for one last victim. The Hypnotist searches the audience again *(again all clowns volunteer)* and selects his third victim. Victim 3 smugly approaches the stage and takes a seat. There is no way he can be hypnotized. No, sir. The Hypnotist asks for silence and begins circling his wand in Victim 3's face. He circles to the right. No response. Victim 3 indicates, "See, I told you so." Not giving up, the Hypnotist circles the wand to the left. Still no response. So he tries circling the wand twice as fast as normal, but still Victim 3 remains wide awake. Aha! The Hypnotist has an idea! He reaches behind the chair and holds the foam bat above Victim 3's head (quite unknown to Victim 3!) After indicating to the audience not to reveal his secret, the Hypnotist hits Victim 3 soundly on the head with the foam bat. And Victim 3 immediately is asleep.

Now, what would be an appropriate action for this victim? Hmmmm. The Hypnotist strokes his chin in deep thought and at last has a great idea! He indicates that he will cause Victim 3 to begin kissing members of the audience! The Hypnotist rings the bell in Victim 3's ear. He rises slowly, raises his eyebrows, or winks several times at someone in the audience; and then begins approaching them making kissing motions. *(Victim 3 goes directly into the audience and pretends to kiss several members.)* After a few kisses, the Hypnotist blows the whistle. Victim 3 turns back toward the Hypnotist, but instead of stopping the action, he continues kissing and begins chasing the Hypnotist! The Hypnotist frantically continues blowing the whistle with Victim 3, still in a trance, chasing after him. They circle the stage and then run offstage.

(NOTE: If this skit is part of a longer program of routines, the whistle-blowing hypnotist and the kisser chasing him can return to dash across the stage or through the audience between comic acts. Or a ringmaster can hold the bell for safekeeping only to have it fall to the floor later during the program. Upon hearing the bell ring, all the victims from this skit would immediately jump up in the audience and begin doing jumping jacks, acting like a chicken, or kissing people until the ringmaster can locate a whistle to make them stop.)

Prop Notes: You can purchase all props through local department stores or specialty shops, or you can make them inexpensively from other materials. Make the magic wand from a ¾-inch dowel stick approximately 12 inches long and paint it black with white tips. You can substitute a rolled newspaper (comics section, of course!) for the foam bat.

THE CHOIR

(Written in collaboration with Kelly Hunsucker.)

TYPE OF SKIT: Inspirational

THEME: Always strive to do your best. "Do your best to present yourself to God as one approved" (2 Tim. 2:15).

TARGET AUDIENCE: Children (See "Adapting for All Age Groups" following skit outline for suggestions for youth and adults.)

LENGTH OF SKIT: Four to seven minutes

CAST OF CLOWNS: Director
Clown
Four to five Choir Members

PROPS: Songbooks
Director's baton
Small spray bottle
Sign: You Need to Practice
(See Prop Notes following skit outline.)

The Choir enters carrying songbooks, forms a semicircle, and continues talking among themselves and warming up their vocal chords. The Director, a refined and somewhat serious character, enters dramatically and takes a bow, acknowledging the audience. The Choir snaps to attention as the Director takes his place. The Director turns a few pages in his songbook and, using his fingers, announces to the choir the number of the selection to be performed. They turn the pages in their songbooks and stand poised for the downbeat. The Director raises his baton and gives the downbeat, and the concert begins. *(As the downbeat is given, members of the Choir, acting very professionally, begin mouthing the words to a song such as "Jesus Loves Me," "Happy Birthday" [for birthday occasions], a Christmas carol [for the holiday season], or any other song—as long as all members are miming the same one!)* Ah! The choir is in top form and the Director is well pleased!

The Clown enters from the side, hears the beautiful music, and stops to enjoy the melodious strains. He indicates to the audience that he, too, is a wonderful singer and is going to try to join the Choir. He gets his confidence up and strides over to the Director, tapping him on the shoulder and asking for a chance to sing in the choir. The Director is annoyed at having to stop the Choir, and the Choir members are equally annoyed. The Clown pleads and convinces the Director to allow him to join the choir. The Director gives the Clown a songbook and the Clown quickly takes his place with the Choir. He inquires as to the number of the selection and one or two Choir members relay the message. The Clown frantically thumbs through the pages of his songbook and indicates he has now found the correct page.

Once again, the Director gives the downbeat and the singing begins. The Choir sings as professionally as before, but the Clown's singing is obviously loud and obnoxious. He flails his arms high into the air, and begins dancing about making a spectacle of himself. The Choir is shocked. One by one they stop singing and stare at the Clown. The Director covers his ears and stomps his feet in disgust. He moves toward the Clown, snaps the songbook from his hands, and points his baton to the side of the stage, indicating that the Clown must leave. The Clown is hurt and hangs his head as he walks away, turning back once or twice to ask for another chance which, of course, the Director refuses to give him. The Clown moves to the side of the stage, but not out of sight of the audience.

The Director straightens himself, gains his composure, and takes his place once again in front of the Choir. He again gives the downbeat and the Choir begins singing. Still off to the side, the Clown indicates that he has an idea! He pulls out a spray bottle and sprays his throat. He tries a few notes. Say, that's pretty good! Now, he's ready to give it another try. Mustering his courage, the Clown returns to the Choir asking the Director for a second chance. As the Clown tugs at the Director's sleeve, the Director is angered at having to stop the Choir yet again. Reluctantly, the Director lets the Clown back in the Choir and the business of finding the correct page takes place. The Clown checks the page number with the Choir member next to him, and receives an emphatic answer from the entire Choir in unison. The Director again gives the downbeat and the Choir begins to sing. The Clown begins his outrageous singing (not to mention his dance moves) and, again, it is awful. The Director asks him to leave, a little more forcefully this time. After every few steps, the Clown looks back at the Director, who waves him farther and farther away. Again, the Clown stands to the side, hurt and rejected.

One member of the Choir notices the Clown and feels sorry for him. He slips out of position carrying a sign that says, You Need to Practice, and hands it to the Clown. Practice? What a concept! The Clown decides to give it a try and begins practicing off to the side while the Choir member slips back into place. At last, the Clown is ready to try again. He is confident as he returns to the Director and asks for just one more chance. After some amount of pleading and after several refusals, the Director gives in and agrees to let the Clown have one last chance. This time as the Director gives the downbeat, the Clown blends in beautifully with the Choir and sings as professionally as the best of them. One by one, the members of the Choir stop singing and the Director stops conducting, but the Clown continues. When he realizes that everyone is listening to him, he assumes that his singing still is not good enough. He hands his songbook to the choir member beside him, hangs his head, and starts to leave. But instead of sending him away, the Choir members begin applauding him and lead the audience in applause as well.

Adapting for All Age Groups: This skit works well as is with all age groups but can be adapted slightly to meet different interests by making the following changes:

For Youth: Change the song being mouthed by the Choir to "Pass It On," "Sweet, Sweet Spirit," or another favorite youth hymn for use in church settings; or use an easy-listening, popular song easily recognizable by youth in other settings. For use in more secular settings, transform the Choir itself into a rock band using inflatable instruments, with the Director being replaced by a lead guitarist or lead singer. If you make this change, make sure that the actions of the Band do not overshadow the overacting and bad playing (singing) of the clown trying to join in. If you use a band concept rather than a choir, eliminate the indication by the Choir of the correct number to be performed and replace it with the band leader humming a few bars of a song until the clown identifies it as one he knows! Also, replace the scenario with the clown spraying his throat with the polishing of an instrument or the changing of guitar strings, etc.

For Adults: Younger adults will respond well either to the Choir scenario or the adaptation for youth shown above. Middle-aged adults and senior adults may have a better response to the Choir setting. Change the mouthed song to "Amazing Grace" or another easily identifiable lyric for a church setting. This age group may be less likely to identify with "moonwalking" or modern dance moves but can easily make the connection to exaggerated footwork, "disco" arms, and boisterous singing styles.

Prop Notes: Make songbooks from colored folders with the word *Songbook* written on the front, or use ordinary hymnals or other songbooks as long as all books are the same. Make a director's baton from a ½-inch dowel stick about 12 inches long and paint it either gold or silver. Small spray bottles are available at most department stores. Make the You Need to Practice sign at least 10-by-14 inches and laminate or coat it with clear adhesive covering.

If you choose the option for youth and substitute the concept of a band for the choir, purchase inflatable guitars, saxophones, and other instruments from novelty shops or mail order catalogs.

COLOR-BLIND

TYPE OF SKIT: Inspirational

THEME: We are to love others without prejudice.
"Dear friends, since God so loved us, we also ought to love one another" (1 John 4:11).
"This is my command: Love each other" (John 15:17).

TARGET AUDIENCE: Children (See "Adapting for All Age Groups" following skit outline for suggestions for youth and adults)

LENGTH OF SKIT: Four to seven minutes

CAST OF CLOWNS: Blue Clown
Yellow Clown
Blue Group (one to three)
Yellow Group (one to three)

PROPS: Two large signs (one No Blue; one No Yellow; see illustration on p. 53)
Two large double-sided squares with string attached (blue on one side and yellow on the other)
Three large blue squares with string attached. Three large yellow squares with string attached
Beachball
Blowing bubbles
Oversized blue and yellow crayons
Two chairs
(See Prop Notes following skit outline.)

SETUP: The two chairs are arranged side-by-side about 12 inches apart at center stage. The oversized blue crayon is placed on the side of the stage where the Yellow Group will be clowning; and the oversized yellow crayon is placed on the side of the stage where the Blue Group will be clowning. The Blue Clown will wear a two-sided square around his neck with the blue side showing, and the Yellow Clown will wear the other two-sided square with the yellow side showing. These clowns become a part of the group of the same color and participate in all Group activities indicated in the skit. When individual action is required, they will be referred to as either the Blue Clown or the Yellow Clown. All other clowns will be divided into two groups: one group will wear blue squares around their necks and the other group will wear yellow squares.

The Blue Group enters from one side of the stage laughing, talking, and having a grand time. One member of the group is carrying a beachball and another is carrying the No Yellow sign. The Yellow Group enters from the opposite side of the stage, also laughing, talking, and having a wonderful time. One member of that group is carrying a bottle of blowing bubbles and another is carrying the No Blue sign. As the two groups reach center stage and see each other, they both stop short. The Blue Group gives the Yellow Group the once-over and the Yellow Group does the same to the Blue Group.

One of the Blue Group members (but *not* the Blue Clown) takes the No Yellow sign and smugly approaches the chairs at center stage. A member from the Yellow Group (but *not* the Yellow Clown) does the same. The two clowns stare at one another with obvious distaste. The Blue Group member props his No Yellow sign on one of the chairs and stands with his arms crossed in satisfaction. So, there! The Yellow Group member saunters over and props his No Blue sign on the other chair and likewise crosses his arms. Humph! The two clowns snub each other and walk back to their respective groups.

As they return to their groups, they notice that the Blue Clown and the Yellow Clown are waving at each other from across the stage. Well! They certainly can't have that! They drag the Blue Clown and the Yellow Clown off to their respective groups—the Blue Group on one side of the stage and the Yellow Group on the other.

Let the games begin! The Blue Group begins tossing their beachball and the Yellow Group begins blowing and chasing bubbles. Each group seems to be having a wonderful time. The Yellow Clown sneaks away from the bubble-blowing activity and inches his way a little closer to the chairs. He waves at the Blue Clown. Unfortunately, the Blue Clown takes his attention off the beachball game to shyly wave back and gets hit in the head with the ball! *Ouch!* That hurt. The Blue Clown indicates that his head hurts and that he will just wait over near the chairs while the others continue playing. Once the others have returned to their playing, the Blue Clown moves as close to the invisible boundary line as possible, wipes his sweaty palm on his pants, bends, and stretches to extend a handshake to the Yellow Clown, careful not to cross the chair line where no Blue is allowed. The Yellow Clown attempts to return the gesture. He wipes his own sweaty palm, bends and stretches to extend a handshake to the Blue Clown — also being careful not to cross the chair line where no Yellow is allowed. But, alas, no matter how hard they try, their hands do not quite meet.

As the Yellow and Blue Clowns are attempting a handshake, their respective Group members spot the action. Oh, no! We certainly can't have a Blue Clown and a Yellow Clown being friends! The Blue Group grabs the Blue Clown and drags him back to their area and the Yellow Group does the same with the Yellow Clown. Once again, the play activities begin with the Blue Clown and the Yellow Clown joining in halfheartedly. Then at exactly the same moment *(action must be synchronized)* they both get an idea! (But quite unknown to each other!) The Blue Clown sneaks to the side and gets the yellow crayon and shows it to the audience. At the same time, the Yellow Clown sneaks to the opposite side and gets the blue crayon and shows it to the audience. Both clowns indicate that they are going to change the color of their square so that they can play with the other.

The Blue Clown removes the square from around his neck being careful not to reveal the yellow side to the audience and the Yellow Clown removes his square being careful not to reveal the blue side. The two clowns either sit or kneel on the stage holding their squares propped in front of them so that the original colors are facing out. Each takes a crayon and begins feverishly coloring the backside of their squares. When they complete the coloring, they turn the squares so that the audience sees the new and opposite colors. *(This action also should be synchronized.)* The two clowns put on the new colored squares and both hurry back to the chairs. Just as they near the chairs, both clowns skid to a halt as they notice that their plan has not worked. Oh, no! They are *still* opposite colors!

Just as the two clowns are considering their dilemma, the Blue Group sees the Yellow Clown (who is now wearing the blue square) and, thinking him to be the Blue Clown, they grab him and drag him back to the beachball game. Likewise, the Yellow Group sees the Blue Clown (who is now wearing the yellow square) and thinks he is the Yellow Clown. They grab him and drag him back to the bubble-blowing game.

After the games have begun once again, the Blue Clown and the Yellow Clown both sadly walk away from their groups and toward the chairs. They look at the No Blue and No Yellow signs, wave sorrowfully to each other, and then hang their heads solemnly.

Aha! The Blue Clown has an idea! He claps his hands to get the attention of the Yellow Clown and expresses his joy in solving their dilemma. At the sound of the clapping hands, the Blue Group and the Yellow Group both stop their activity and curiously watch what is going on. The Blue Clown removes his square and throws it behind the chairs. Ta-da! No color at all now! The Yellow Clown agrees. What a great idea! He also removes his square and throws it behind the chairs. At last, they are the same! The two clowns embrace as good friends in front of the chairs.

The Blue Group and the Yellow Group are a bit confused at first, but one by one, they, too,

Sample
No Blue/No Yellow Sign

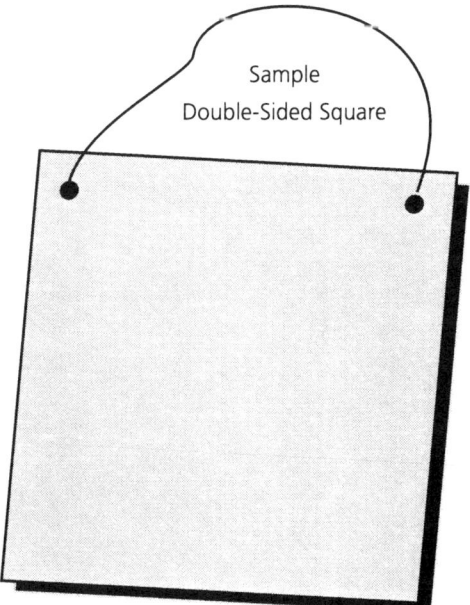

Sample
Double-Sided Square

remove their colored squares. The two groups now intermingle, shaking hands and greeting one another with love, forming one large group. As the large group leaves the stage, still laughing and talking, the Blue Clown and the Yellow Clown look at the signs on the chairs. The Blue Clown picks up the No Yellow sign and the Yellow Clown picks up the No Blue sign. They look at each other, and then both tear the signs in half, tossing the pieces aside and leaving the stage arm in arm.

Adapting for All Age Groups: Because of its simple message, this skit works well with all age groups. However, make it more age-appropriate for groups that may not contain children with the following changes:

For Youth: Change the activities the two groups do to something more identifiable with teenagers, such as listening to the radio, tossing a Frisbee, playing tennis, etc.

For Adults: Change the activities the two groups do to reflect prejudicial situations for adults. For example, one group could be reading the *Wall Street Journal* and counting their large wads of money, while the other could be working with farming implements.

Prop Notes: Make the No Blue and No Yellow signs on poster board. Do not laminate these, as they will be torn at the conclusion of the skit. Make the large blue and yellow squares from construction paper about 10-by-10 inches with string attached in lengths that allow the squares to be hung easily around the neck. Laminate these squares or coat them with clear adhesive covering to allow for prolonged use and storage. Two of the squares need to be double-sided with blue on one side and yellow on the other. A beachball and blowing bubbles are inexpensive items and you can purchase them at any department store. Purchase the oversized crayons or make them from inexpensive materials (see "Portrait Perils").

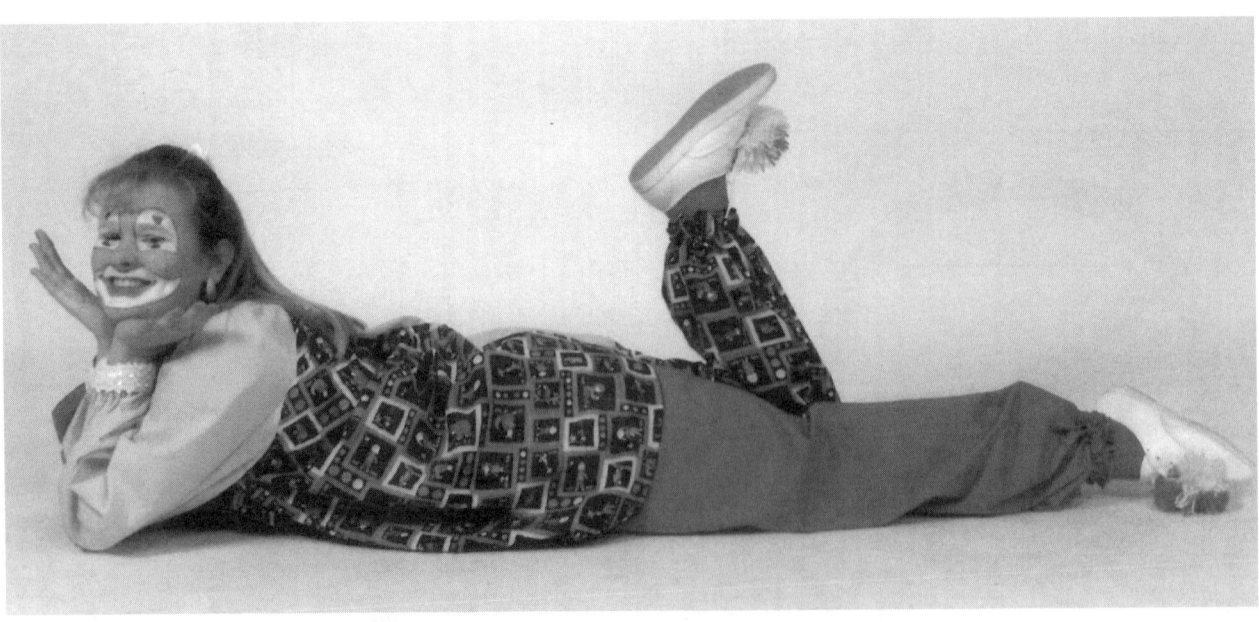

"IT AIN'T HEAVY... I HAVE A BROTHER"

TYPE OF SKIT: Inspirational

THEME: We are to help others and show Jesus' love to them by sharing their burdens.
"Carry each others burdens, and in this way you will fulfill the law of Christ" (Gal. 6:2).

TARGET AUDIENCE: Youth (See "Adapting for All Age Groups" following skit outline for suggestions for adults and children.)

LENGTH OF SKIT: Six to ten minutes

CAST OF CLOWNS: The Boss
The Worker
Nail File Clown (Female)
Two Laughing Clowns
Friend

PROPS: Large packing box marked with the words *Cares and Woe Packing Company*
Six other small boxes of varying sizes (to fit inside the large packing box), each marked with one of the following: *Loneliness, Guilt, Fear, Peer Pressure, Family Problems, Disappointment*
Large handkerchief
Oversized nail file
Two empty soda cans
(See Prop Notes following skit outline.)

SETUP: Place the large packing box to one side of the stage with the smaller boxes nearby. (Note: The words marked on each box should not be visible to the audience.)

The Boss enters with his arm around the shoulders of the Worker as if he's showing him the ropes of the packing and moving business. He indicates to the Worker that the large packing box needs to be moved over to the loading area at the other side of the stage. The Worker is confident that he can handle the job and indicates so to the audience. This is going to be a piece of cake! The Worker rolls up his sleeves ready for a hard day's work and heads toward the large box. The Boss, with his hands on his hips and shaking his head, watches the obviously inexperienced Worker. "This guy sure doesn't know much about the packing and moving business," the Boss thinks. The Worker very easily picks up the large, empty box and starts toward the loading area with it. As he gets about halfway across the stage, the Boss nonchalantly steps in front of him, holds out a hand, hitting the box and stopping the Worker dead in his tracks.

No, no, no. Not the *empty* box. The Boss points to the pile of smaller boxes, indicating they are to be packed into the larger one before it is moved.

Good grief! The Worker hits the heel of his hand against the side of his head at his own ignorance. Of course, the smaller boxes go *inside* the larger one. What was he thinking? He takes the large box and follows the Boss back to the stack of smaller boxes. The Worker eyeballs the stack of smaller boxes, sizes them up and visually measures to see if they will fit into the larger box. Obviously, they will fit easily—this job is *still* going to be a piece of cake! The Worker puts the large box on the floor and opens the top. He brushes his hands together as he readies himself to load the smaller boxes.

While the Worker is getting ready, the Boss has already picked up the first two of the smaller boxes, one stacked on top of the other. (NOTE: *Smaller boxes should be loaded in order of size, smallest first. Also, the signs depicting the various burdens should be in plain sight of the audience as they are brought out.*) Despite their smaller size, the boxes are quite heavy, and the Boss has some difficulty getting them over to the Worker. The Worker is a little confused by the excessive weight of such small objects, but holds out his hands to receive the boxes. After all, how heavy can two small boxes be? As the Boss places the boxes into the Worker's hands, his arms drop suddenly toward the floor under the weight. Wait a minute! These are *really* heavy. With some degree of difficulty, the Worker at last heaves the smaller boxes into the larger one. He pants a few times and turns to find the Boss returning with the third and fourth small, but terribly heavy, boxes again stacked on top of each other.

All right. The Worker is braced and ready now. He spits on the palms of his hands waiting to receive the small boxes. The Worker squints his eyes, anticipating the force of the weight. *Oof!* The Boss drops the boxes into the Worker's hands and again he packs them in the larger box—but with some difficulty.

While the Worker is loading the third and fourth boxes, the Boss drags the fifth box (a little larger than the first four) out onto the stage and leaves it right beside the Worker. As the Worker finishes putting the third and fourth small boxes into the packing crate, he turns and trips over the fifth box. *Ouch!* My toe! The Worker bounces around on one foot while holding the other in total agony! After giving a dirty look in the direction of the Boss (who by this time has returned to the pile of small boxes), the Worker tries to lift the smaller box.

It only moves a few inches from the floor; and although he must remain in a bent-over position to do so, the Worker is able to just barely lift it and move it over to the packing box—muttering under his breath several obviously negative comments about his satisfaction with the situation!

Uh-oh! The Worker has arrived at the packing box—but he is still bent over and can't seem to get the smaller box high enough to go inside the larger one. He looks at the large box. Then at the audience. Then down at the smaller box. Then back to the audience. After rolling his eyes in thought, he begins slowly swinging his arms in a back and forth motion, moving the smaller box slightly higher with each swing. One, two, three! *Kerplunk!* The smaller box falls into the larger one and the Worker covers his ears as if hearing the sound of breaking glass! *Oops!*

While this activity has been going on, the Boss has been slowly moving the last and heaviest of the smaller boxes toward the Worker. He stops every few steps and takes out a handkerchief to wipe the perspiration from his forehead. The Worker turns to see the Boss with this latest heavy object. *Whoa!* He does a double take and stumbles back a step or two.

The Boss is pooped and needs to rest. So he indicates to the Worker that he should put this last box into the larger packing box. The Worker points at the smaller box with disbelief. *That* box? Are you kidding? But the Boss isn't kidding and leaves the scene panting and wiping his forehead.

Wait! Don't go! The Worker points to the retreating Boss, then to the heavy box, back to the retreating Boss, the box, the disappearing Boss . . . and finally looks sorrowfully at the audience.

Hmmm. What a dilemma. But wait! The Worker has an idea! He gets behind the box and bends over to push it. (*There is much ado about this with the box moving only inches at a time. If possible, give the illusion of pushing against the box with the hands while the feet slide out backwards slightly.)* After a great deal of effort, the Worker moves the box inch by inch until it is close enough to the packing box and he begins the ordeal of trying to get it inside. He tries to lift the box, but it is impossible.

About this time, the Nail File Clown enters walking across the stage snapping her chewing gum and filing and admiring her lovely nails. Hey! The Worker indicates that he could use some help. Hey! Over here! The Nail File Clown gives a "Who, me?" expression to which the Worker indicates his need for help in lifting the box. The Nail File Clown holds her hand out admiringly. Are you nuts? I'd break a nail. Sorry. And the Nail File Clown saunters away.

Again, the Worker ponders the situation and tries to lift the heavy box, but to no avail. As his frustration builds, the Worker kicks the box, hurting his toe once again and he hops around in pain. Two Laughing Clowns enter, talking and sipping from soda cans as they cross the stage.

Hey! Hey, you! The Worker tries to get their attention. At last, the Laughing Clowns notice him and the Worker is able to explain his dilemma and ask for their assistance. The Laughing Clowns look seriously at the Worker, then at the box, back at the Worker, and then at each other. They burst into raucous laughter. Are you crazy? It's break time! And the Laughing Clowns exit.

The Worker waves after them to try and get their attention, but he ends up all alone again with his heavy box. Just as the Worker begins to quiver his bottom lip and sadly hangs his head, the Friend appears on the scene. The Friend notices the Worker and immediately feels sorry for him. He approaches the Worker to see what the problem is. The Worker tearfully (and quite dramatically) explains his problem as the Friend listens. The Friend suggests that perhaps if they *both* worked together, they could lift the heavy box. The Worker beams! What a great idea! You'd do that for me? Thanks!

The Friend and the Worker each take a side of the heavy box. On the count of three, they lift. Although the box is heavy and it takes some doing, the two of them are able to lift it into the packing box. Phew! What a job! Both the Friend and the Worker lean exhaustedly on the large box.

With the job completed, the Friend offers a handshake to the Worker. As the Friend tries to leave, the Worker won't let go of his hand. The Worker takes on a sad expression and indicates that now he must move the entire large packing box over to the loading area at the other side of the stage.

The Friend looks at the box and at the large distance to the loading area. *This* box? Over *there?* The Friend scratches his head in thought. Then he rolls up his sleeves and indicates, "Come on, let's do it!" The Worker is elated and both of them get behind the large packing box, pushing it toward the loading area.

The two successfully move the box to the other side of the stage. The Worker and the Friend wipe their foreheads, then shake hands, put their arms around each other's shoulders, and exit happily.

Adapting for All Age Groups: Make a few minor changes in this skit to make it age-appropriate for adults or for children.

For Adults: Change the words on the smaller boxes to *Loneliness, Grief, Financial Worries, Family Problems, Loss of Job, Temptation.*

For Children: The subtleties of labeling the smaller boxes may be lost on an audience of children, particularly if they have not yet learned to read. Children need to receive the basic concept of sharing burdens and helping one another without the confusing addition of labels that may or may not be understood. Simply use plain boxes for this audience.

Prop Notes: Use a variety of sizes and colors for boxes. Make the large packing box plain with only the words *Cares and Woe Packing Company* printed on the side. Make the signs for the smaller boxes and attach them with either tape or hook and loop fasteners, thus making them interchangeable enough to meet the needs of different age groups or so that you can use the boxes without labels if desired. Make an oversized handkerchief from brightly colored fabric or purchase a bandanna. Make the oversized nail file from either a thin board of plastic foam or cardboard and paint it brown on one side and blue or pink on the other. While the oversized nail file brings more laughs, the ordinary kind works just as well. Be sure to clean empty soda cans thoroughly and file any sharp edges to prevent injury.

OOEY-GOOEY

(An original variation of the classic "Sin Box" skit. Author unknown.)

TYPE OF SKIT: Message

THEME: Our sinful nature often lands us in some sticky situations. But God will forgive us when we confess our sins and ask for His forgiveness.
"For all have sinned and fall short of the Glory of God" (Rom. 3:23).
"If we confess our sins, he is faithful and just and will forgive us our sins and purify us from all unrighteousness"(1 John 1:9).

TARGET AUDIENCE: Youth and adults

LENGTH OF SKIT: Four to seven minutes

CAST OF CLOWNS: Wallpaper Clown
　　　　　　　　Assistant
　　　　　　　　Curious Clown

PROPS: Chair (or table)
　　　　Wide paintbrush
　　　　Large plastic bucket marked *Glue*
　　　　Roll of wallpaper
　　　　Two lunch bags
　　　　Out to Lunch Sign
　　　　Double-sided sign: The words *Do Not Touch* printed on one side and the word *Sin* printed on the other
　　　　Bible
　　　　(See Prop Notes following skit outline.)

SETUP: The Wallpaper Clown and his Assistant are on the scene setting up the glue can, the paintbrush, and measuring the wallpaper, etc. Arrange these props on a chair or table to make them more visible. Prop the Bible behind the chair or table.

The Wallpaper Clown and his Assistant are busily arranging their supplies and measuring wallpaper to be placed on an imaginary wall. The Curious Clown enters and acknowledges the audience by waving and drawing their attention to the activity of the Wallpaper Clown and his Assistant. Hopefully, the audience is as curious about what is going on as the Curious Clown.

The Curious Clown moves closer to where the other clowns are working. Maybe they will even let him help! While the Wallpaper

Clown and the Assistant are holding the wallpaper up to the imaginary wall to see how it will look, the Curious Clown spots the glue can. He points it out to the audience and then moves closer to it. After sneaking a quick peek inside, he touches the edge of the bucket. Ooey-gooey! The Curious Clown rubs his fingers together. Boy, this stuff is sticky! The Wallpaper Clown spots the Curious Clown beside the glue bucket and tells him to leave. This is no place for an amateur! The Curious Clown wipes his sticky fingers on his pants and moves away—but only a short distance, still watching all the action. He stands off to the side *(still in view of the audience)*, whistling and trying to act innocent and nonchalant. Every now and then, he takes a quick glance toward the decorating supplies, snapping back to his innocent whistling each time the Wallpaper Clown looks in his direction.

The Assistant checks his watch. Hey, look! He taps the Wallpaper Clown on the back to give him the news. It's time for lunch! The Wallpaper Clown checks his own watch. By George, you're right! The Wallpaper Clown and the Assistant put down their tools of the trade and grab their lunch bags, preparing to leave. The Assistant brings out an Out to Lunch sign and props it against the decorating supplies. That should do it. The Assistant and the Wallpaper Clown take a few more steps and then the Assistant stops short. *(The Assistant should be in front of the two exiting clowns so that when he stops the Wallpaper Clown bumps into him.)* Look at that! The Assistant points to the Curious Clown. Now, what is *that* guy up to?

Wait! The Assistant knows just what to do. He returns to the supply area and brings out another sign. This one reads *Do Not Touch*. He props the sign *(being careful not to reveal the* Sin *printed on the opposite side)* beside the glue and paper. Then, brushing his hands together in satisfaction, he gives an assuring nod to the Wallpaper Clown, and they leave for their lunch break.

The Curious Clown carefully checks around to be sure no one can see him. Are they gone? Shh! The audience must be very quiet! He tiptoes over a little closer to the supplies, then double-checks to be sure no one is coming. A few more tiptoe steps and another check. A few more steps and he's right at the supplies. Certainly, *he* is as smart as those professionals and can put up the wallpaper while the other clowns are away. The Curious Clown picks up the Do Not Touch sign *(being careful not to reveal the* Sin *printed on the opposite side)* and reads it. Nah! That can't possibly mean him! So, he lays the sign aside *(with the* Sin *side down)* and picks up the wallpaper and rolls out a length, laying it on the floor (or table if one is available.)

Now for the glue. The Curious Clown points toward the glue bucket and then moves toward it. He takes the paintbrush and dips it in the can of glue. It takes a little effort to get the brush back out. Ooey-gooey! Holding the brush with the tips of his fingers, the Curious Clown moves toward the wallpaper piece. He places one hand on the paper and begins brushing with the other.

Not watching what he is doing, the Curious Clown accidentally brushes the glue over his hand! Yuck! He tries shaking the glue off. Still gooey. He tries rubbing one hand with the other. Now *both* hands are gooey! He tries shaking both hands and as he does so, he loses his balance and knocks the entire bucket of glue over onto the floor. Oh, no! What a mess! The Curious Clown steps over to clean it up and gets his foot stuck fast to the floor in the pile of glue. He dares not touch anything with his sticky hands, but still tries his best to free his foot. Rats! It just won't budge.

Uh-oh! The Curious Clown hears someone coming. Oh, no! It's the Wallpaper Clown and the Assistant returning from their lunch and he still can't budge his foot. What *will* he do? As the Wallpaper Clown and the Assistant come into view, the Curious Clown quickly strikes a pose placing one hand on his hip and holding his chin with the other hand as if he is contemplating a deep thought. He begins whistling as if nothing is wrong.

The Wallpaper Clown and the Assistant see the mess and are outraged. What happened here?! They both point accusingly at the Curious Clown. You! Did *you* do this? They question the Curious Clown about the incident, and as he tries to indicate that he knows nothing about it, he realizes that not only is his foot stuck to the floor, but now his hands are stuck to his body as well! It certainly doesn't take long for the Wallpaper Clown and the Assistant to figure out what happened.

The Assistant retrieves the Do Not Touch sign and shows it to the Curious Clown *(without revealing the* Sin *side)* and asks if he indeed touched the supplies. The Curious Clown admits that he did. How humiliating! The Assistant then reveals the back side of the sign reading *Sin* to the audience and then to the Curious Clown. Upon seeing the sign and realizing his mistake, the Curious Clown hangs his head in shame.

The Wallpaper Clown and the Assistant try to help the Curious Clown get unglued. One pulls on an arm while the other pulls on his foot. They change places and try the procedure from a different angle. Needless to say, this is not a pleasant experience for the Curious Clown! And no matter what they try, the Curious Clown will not come unglued.

Aha! The Wallpaper Clown has an idea and goes to retrieve the Bible. After showing the audience what he has brought, he begins reading. After some amount of flamboyant page turning, he locates just the information he needs. He shows the passage to the Assistant who nods in agreement about the solution. The Wallpaper Clown and the Assistant kneel to pray, one on each side of the Curious Clown. As they pray, they point toward the Curious Clown and his predicament. While the praying is going on, lo and behold, one of the Curious Clown's hands comes unglued. He wiggles it about, delighted with the new-found freedom. Then the second hand is released, and finally even his foot is free! Oh, happy day!

The Wallpaper Clown and the Assistant close their prayers with a visibly mouthed "Amen" and look up excitedly to find that the Curious Clown is now unstuck. The Curious Clown is dancing for joy and raises his arms toward heaven with a big "Thank You!" He grabs the hand of the Wallpaper Clown and shakes it vigorously to express his gratitude. Then the Curious Clown acts as though his hand is stuck to the Wallpaper Clown's hand and that he can't let go. For a moment, all three clowns stop moving and look confused and panicked. "Gotcha! Just kidding!" The Curious Clown releases the handshake revealing that all is well, and the Wallpaper Clown, the Assistant, and the Curious Clown all leave as friends.

Concluding Thought (youth and adults): As human beings, it is our nature to be sinful, and often we find ourselves caught in a sticky situation—all because we made a bad choice. We may have chosen to do what *we* wanted to do without thinking how our actions might affect someone else. Or maybe we chose to follow the crowd instead of following God. But there's good news! God knows that we are sinners and in spite of that, He still loves us. If we confess our sins to Him and ask forgiveness, God will forgive us and give us a fresh start.
(Option: For an audience of youth or adults, conclude the skit simply by reading 1 John 1:9.)

Prop Notes: Use an old paintbrush rather than purchasing an expensive new one. Purchase a roll of out-of-stock wallpaper; or perhaps a local building contractor might donate an extra roll. Make the glue bucket from a large plastic ice-cream container with a wire handle. Cover the bucket with adhesive paper and print the word *Glue* in large letters on two sides. Stuff the lunch bags with tissue paper to give the illusion of fullness. Make the Out to Lunch sign and the double-sided Do Not Touch/Sin sign from poster board at least 10-by-14 inches. Laminate or coat the signs with clear adhesive covering.

THE PESKY FLY

TYPE OF SKIT: Message

THEME: God has shown mercy to us and we are to show mercy to others.
"In his great mercy he has given us new birth into a living hope through the resurrection of Jesus Christ from the dead" (1 Peter 1:3).
"Be merciful, just as your Father is merciful" (Luke 6:36).

TARGET AUDIENCE: Youth and adults (concluding thought adapted for use with older children)

LENGTH OF SKIT: Three to five minutes

CAST OF CLOWNS: Annoyed Clown
Sleeping Clown
Bible Clown

PROPS: Two chairs
Comics
Large flyswatter
Squirt gun
Bible
Plastic jar with lid
(See Prop Notes following skit outline.)

SETUP: Place two chairs center stage with the large flyswatter and the plastic jar with lid behind them. The Sleeping Clown has the squirt gun either hidden inside a deep pocket or behind one of the chairs.

The Sleeping Clown sits slouched in one chair, with the Annoyed Clown reading comics in the other. The Bible Clown is on the floor propped up on his elbows and knees, cupping his chin in his hands, and reading the Bible.

What's that? The Annoyed Clown hears a buzzing sound and is distracted from his reading. His eyes and head follow the flight pattern of the annoying insect. Oh, no! It's a pesky fly! Still seated, the Annoyed Clown swats at the air several times trying to get rid of the pest. Not having any luck, he stands and begins swatting more furiously, missing each and every time and getting rather exasperated with the whole ordeal. For a moment, the Annoyed Clown stops moving, narrows his eyes, and follows the fly as he slowly and purposefully rolls up the comics even tighter than before. He is determined to get rid of this pest!

Wait! What's this? It's almost too funny! The Annoyed Clown has followed the fly and found that it has landed on the head of the Sleeping Clown. Shh! Everyone must be very quiet. He just can't miss this time. The Annoyed Clown takes a few warm-up swings and then lands a blow with his rolled comics directly to the head of the Sleeping Clown. Quite naturally, the Sleeping Clown leaps to his feet, grabbing his sore head. And, boy, is he mad! Quickly calming the Sleeping Clown, the Annoyed Clown points out the pesky fly that is buzzing around the room.

Oh! *Now* the Sleeping Clown understands the situation. Both the Annoyed Clown and the Sleeping Clown begin following the insect with their eyes (*movements should be synchronized*). The Annoyed Clown makes a few more misguided swipes at the air, missing the fly with each swing.

Wait! The Sleeping Clown has an idea! He reaches behind his chair and brings out the large flyswatter and is ready to do battle *(complete with some flexing, deep knee bends, and fencing moves to prepare for the encounter).* He begins swatting wildly in the air, following the fly but constantly missing him.

The Sleeping Clown and his flyswatter end up right behind the Bible Clown, who is quietly reading his Bible, oblivious to the activity around him. Aha! The Sleeping Clown notices that the fly has landed on the rear end of the Bible Clown. He shares this information with the Annoyed Clown and the audience. Shh! Nobody make a sound!

The Sleeping Clown sneaks up behind the Bible Clown and swats at the fly. *(A clap can be made offstage at the point of impact making the swat sound like it hit when actually it does not.)* Ouch! The Bible Clown jumps up and is quite disturbed at the Sleeping Clown's behavior! Just what was *that* all about? The Annoyed Clown and the Sleeping Clown quickly show him the pesky fly buzzing around the room and he seems to understand, although he continues rubbing the stinging spot on his hip.

Now all three clowns stand together following the flight of the fly *(again, motion should be synchronized).* It goes up; it goes down. It makes a long, plummeting spiral and lands right on the nose of the Annoyed Clown. *(The Bible Clown and the Sleeping Clown follow the flight pattern and end up looking at the Annoyed Clown's nose. The Annoyed Clown follows the same pattern and becomes cross-eyed as he follows it to his own nose.)* Shh! The Sleeping Clown knows just what to do. He tiptoes closer to the Annoyed Clown, makes a swooping hand motion toward the Annoyed Clown's face, and triumphantly grabs the fly, holding the captive in his fist. Victory at last! All three clowns are elated that the enemy has been apprehended!

Now that they have caught the fly, what should they do with him? The Annoyed Clown suggests that the fly be thrown mercilessly to the floor, stomped profusely and ground into the dirt. The Sleeping Clown nods vigorously in agreement; but before the action can take place, the Bible Clown frantically waves his arms in disagreement. That would be too cruel! Please don't do that!

The clowns put on their thinking caps again. Aha! Now the Sleeping Clown has an idea. He pulls a squirt gun from his costume (or from behind a chair) and aims it at the fist holding the fly, closing one eye and taking careful aim. The Annoyed Clown nods vigorously in agreement, clapping his hands at the anticipation of the execution to come. Oh, no! The Bible Clown again frantically waves his arms and shakes his head in disagreement. Please! Anything but that! Back to the drawing board, and all three clowns start to think again.

Now, the Bible Clown has an idea. He reaches behind the chairs and produces a jar with a lid, suggesting that the fly be put inside. At first the Annoyed Clown and the Sleeping Clown are not very thrilled with the idea. How boring! But then the Bible Clown indicates that the fly just might run out of air and choke to death. Now, that's more like it! The Annoyed Clown and the Sleeping Clown nod in agreement that this is a good idea. The fly is put into the jar and the lid is closed. The Bible Clown continues to hold the jar while all three clowns stare at it waiting for the pesky fly to get what he deserves. But eventually the Annoyed Clown and then the Sleeping Clown lose interest in the process and decide to leave. The Bible Clown looks carefully around to be sure the other two clowns are out of sight. Then he opens the jar lid and lets the fly go, waving to it as it flies away.

Concluding Thought: We must seem like pesky flies to God at times. We go our own ways without any pattern to our flight and we often land in places we should not be. But even when we're caught in the trap of our own sin, God shows His mercy to us. In fact, God loves us so much that He sent His Son, Jesus, to die on a cross and be raised from the dead so that we could have eternal life—not because we deserve it or because we earned it, but simply because God loves us.

Concluding Thought (*adapted for use with older children*): Sometimes we can be just like that pesky fly that was buzzing around those clowns! We like to do things our way. And sometimes we end up in the wrong place or doing the wrong thing! Even so, God still loves us. In fact, God loves us so much that He sent His Son, Jesus, to be our Savior. And just like the clown that had mercy on the fly and let him go free, God has mercy on us and He forgives us.

Prop Notes: You can purchase oversized flyswatters in novelty shops or mail order catalogs; however, the ordinary, brightly colored variety will work as well. You can purchase the squirt gun from a department store. Use a plastic jar or container with a lid—glass jars break easily and can cause injuries!

WHICH WAY?

TYPE OF SKIT: Message

THEME: Accepting Jesus Christ as Savior is the only way to salvation and eternal life.
"Jesus answered, 'I am the Way and the Truth and the Life. No one comes to the Father except through me'" (John 14:6).

TARGET AUDIENCE: Youth and adults

LENGTH OF SKIT: Six to ten minutes

CAST OF CLOWNS: Traveling Clown
　Robber
　Staggering Clown
　Toll Clown
　Cross Clown
　Sign Clown
　(See casting notes following skit outline.)

PROPS: Map to Salvation and Eternal Life
　Money bag and oversized money
　Squirt gun
　Plastic bottle inside brown bag
　Sign: Avoid the Toll—Come with Me
　Directional (Arrow) Signs:
　　Wide Road
　　Narrow Road
　Street Signs:
　　Repentance Boulevard
　　Corner of Love and Forgiveness
　　Way of the Cross (sign attached to a large cross)
　　Resurrection Street
　　Faith Avenue
　Traffic Signs:
　　Wrong Way
　　Lane Ends 500 Feet
　　Toll Road Ahead
　　Stop
　　Yield
　　Right of Way
　　Resume Safe Speed

SETUP: The Sign Clown stands center stage holding directional signs—one pointing left toward the Wide Road and one pointing right toward the Narrow Road.

(NOTE: *The amount of traveling space available will depend on the facilities at hand. In some cases, the Traveling Clown will be able to move a great distance in one direction before circling back. In others, he may need to make many loops and turns to finish his journey. The Sign Clown will need to adapt to the changing space and position himself accordingly.*)

The Traveling Clown enters the scene and is obviously very excited about the trip he is about to take. He greets the audience, expressing his enthusiasm and showing his intended travel plans by displaying his Map to Salvation and Eternal Life. He carefully unfolds the map and reads it intently, scratching his head in confusion several times. Oh! How silly of him! He turns the map right-side up and continues to plot his route. Pointing to the map and then toward the Sign Clown, he indicates to the audience, "Aha! This must be the way!" The Traveling Clown refolds the map. Well, he tries to refold it at any rate! Those stubborn maps! Nobody can ever get them back the way they were to start with! Oh, well. He does the best he can and puts the map in his pocket or tucks it underneath his arm before setting off toward the Sign Clown.

When the Traveling Clown reaches the Sign Clown, he realizes that he needs to make a decision. He reads the signs. Hmmm. Narrow Road and Wide Road. Decisions, decisions. The Traveling Clown takes a gander to see what's down the Narrow Road, straining to see as far down the road as possible. *(The Sign Clown smiles and uses his head to indicate that the Narrow Road would be the right decision, but the Traveling Clown doesn't seem to notice him.)* Then the Traveling Clown checks to see what might be down the Wide Road in the same manner.

(The Sign Clown becomes a little dismayed and tries to get the Traveling Clown to see that the Narrow Road would be the better choice. Again, his advice goes unnoticed.)
Since the Traveling Clown can't really see much of anything down either road, he is still undecided about what to do. He looks down the Narrow Road, holding his hands up in front of him and closing one eye as if measuring it. *(The Sign Clown smiles, thinking that the Traveling Clown has chosen the Narrow Road.)* Then the Traveling Clown turns toward the Wide Road and goes through the same measuring procedure. *(The Sign Clown again expresses his dismay that the Traveling Clown would even consider the Wide Road.)* Finally, the Traveling Clown takes his hands and places them on his hips. Then he slowly brings them out in front of him still holding the hip measurement steady. He closes one eye and compares the measured hip size to the Narrow Road and then to the Wide Road. No contest. The Wide Road it is! And the Traveling Clown takes his map in hand, makes a sharp turn toward the Wide Road, and begins walking away. *(NOTE: Where space is limited, clowns can walk in a pantomime manner with the legs moving and giving the illusion of walking while the Clown actually moves very little. The Sign Clown is visibly upset over the choice the Traveling Clown has made. He hangs his head, shaking it back and forth as he exits.)*

Not far down the road, the Traveling Clown comes across a large bag of money *(which has been placed there by another clown while the audience's attention was diverted by the Traveling Clown)*. At first, he walks right by the bag, but a few steps later realizes what he has seen, does a double take and returns to check out the situation. He looks around to be sure no one is watching. The coast is clear and he picks up the bag. First, he shakes it. Then he opens the bag and looks inside. Wow! There's a lot of money in there! He shows a few bills to the audience and then hugs the bag, displaying his greed and love for money. Taking the bag, the

Traveling Clown double-checks to be sure no one has seen him and starts walking once again.

As he is walking, the Traveling Clown passes a Wrong Way sign *(held by the Sign Clown who keeps trying to give the Traveling Clown hints about which way to go! Rats! The Traveling Clown passes right by the sign, obviously not heeding its warning. The Sign Clown sighs and exits.)*. The Traveling Clown constantly looks over his shoulder and holds the money bag even closer to protect it. Something just doesn't feel right about this stretch of the road. As he turns his head in one direction, the Robber jumps out at him from the other! As the Robber aims a squirt gun directly at him and demands the money bag, the Traveling Clown has no recourse but to reluctantly hand it over. The Robber grabs the money bag and runs off.

Now the Traveling Clown is left with no money and is quite saddened by his loss. He can't believe it's all gone. All that wonderful money!

The Traveling Clown looks around him but doesn't seem to recognize any of the scenery. He takes out his map to check his location and is quite puzzled that he can't seem to find this place on the map. Where *is* he, anyway? He scratches his head and then moves on, following the road but not knowing where it will lead. Shortly, he passes a Lane Ends 500 Feet sign *(carried by none other than the Sign Clown who is* still *trying to get the Traveling Clown to see the error of his ways! Again, as the Traveling Clown passes by, the Sign Clown simply sighs and exits.)*.

Oh, no! The lane has ended and he has run out of road! *Now*, which way will the Traveling Clown go? He continues walking while looking at the map. The Staggering Clown enters drinking from the bottle in his brown bag. He is obviously inebriated and staggers right into the Traveling Clown knocking both of the clowns to the ground. The Staggering Clown passes out cold. The Traveling Clown shakes his head to regain his composure and as he stands, he notices the Staggering Clown on the ground. Yikes! This guy needs help! The Traveling Clown begins some rather exaggerated CPR techniques to resuscitate the Staggering Clown. At last, the Staggering Clown revives but seems oblivious to what has happened. He offers the brown bag to the Traveling Clown. "Who, me?" The Traveling Clown checks around to see if anyone is looking. Doesn't seem to be anyone. "Sure, why not." He shrugs, accepts the bottle, and takes a swallow. Yuck! That stuff tastes awful! He returns the bag to the Staggering Clown who wipes off the top and takes a swallow himself as he staggers off.

The Traveling Clown wipes off his mouth with his sleeve and spits a few times to get the nasty taste out of his mouth. As he turns to continue on his way, lo and behold, the Sign Clown is back! This time he holds a sign that says Toll Road Ahead. The Traveling Clown checks his pockets and remembers that he doesn't have any money left. *Now* what will he do? Just then, he hears a "Psst." Where did that come from? The Traveling Clown looks all around him for the source of the sound. The Toll Clown appears sneaking stealthily toward the Traveling Clown and holding a sign that says Avoid the Toll—Come with Me. The devious Toll Clown wiggles his index finger motioning for the Traveling Clown to follow him. The Traveling Clown is wary of the Toll Clown, but as he isn't sure where he is anyway, and since he has no money for the toll, he follows. *(The Sign Clown puts down his sign, sighs, and exits.)* After following the Toll Clown a short distance in a rapid pattern of circles and twirls, the Traveling Clown becomes rather dizzy. The Toll Clown laughs at the reeling Traveling Clown and quickly disappears. Holding his head and trying to steady himself, the Traveling Clown looks around in dismay. The road has gotten quite rocky here and he stumbles on the stones as he walks. And his feet ache to boot!

After a few steps, the Traveling Clown has had all he can take. He is exhausted. He stops, hangs his head and begins sobbing. Just at that moment, the Sign Clown jumps out holding a Stop sign in one hand and a Sinner's Detour sign in the other indicating that the Traveling Clown should take the detour. "Who, me?" The Traveling Clown can't understand why the Sign Clown wants to help him, but he is willing to try the detour. Anything is better than being lost! He makes a sharp U-turn and begins walking in the other direction. *(The Sign Clown exits quickly and returns with the Repentance Boulevard sign in one hand and the Yield sign held behind his back, positioning himself just ahead of the approaching Traveling Clown.)* The Traveling Clown reads the street sign and the Sign Clown brings the Yield sign out from behind his back, showing it to the Traveling Clown. "Who, me?" the Traveling Clown asks. The Sign Clown nods a vigorous "Yes, you."

The Traveling Clown kneels to pray and the Sign Clown smiles as he lovingly looks on. Following the prayer, the Sign Clown motions for the Traveling Clown to move forward. *(He then quickly exits and returns with the Corner of Love and Forgiveness sign, standing a few steps away from the approaching Traveling Clown).* As the Traveling Clown passes the Corner of Love and Forgiveness sign, the Sign Clown smiles broadly and keeps encouraging him to move in the right direction. *(During this action, the Cross Clown enters and positions himself just a few feet from the Sign Clown. He is holding a large*

SAMPLE STREET SIGN

DIRECTIONAL SIGNS

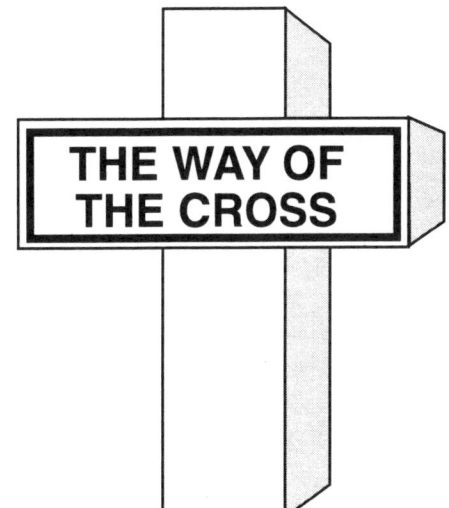

cardboard cross with The Way of the Cross street sign attached. The cross should be as large as possible and resemble a wooden structure. A real cross with the street sign attached could be used in place of the Cross Clown if one is available.)

The Traveling Clown approaches the Cross Clown and slows his pace, looking worshipfully at the cross. He bows his head in reverence. *(During this action, the Sign Clown positions himself on the other side of the Cross Clown and holds the Resurrection Way street sign and a Right-of-Way traffic sign.)* As the Traveling Clown concludes his worship at the cross, the Sign Clown motions for him, leading him in the right direction.

The Traveling Clown reads the street sign. The Sign Clown points to the Right-of-Way sign and gives the go-ahead to the Traveling Clown. Now, he is ready to travel and steps out on his course with confidence! His arms are swinging by his side, his head is held high, and he is whistling a merry tune. *(The Sign Clown exits and returns with the Faith Avenue and Resume Safe Speed signs, positioning himself just a few feet ahead of the approaching Traveling Clown.)* As the Traveling Clown nears the Faith Avenue sign, the Sign Clown no longer has to motion him on. He simply stands there waving at the Traveling Clown. Still whistling, and not stopping any longer than for time to return a joyous wave to the Sign Clown, the Traveling Clown moves on.

Concluding Thought: Jesus said, "I am the Way and the Truth and the Life. No one comes to the Father except through me." God loves us very much and has provided a way for us to have abundant eternal life. All we have to do is realize that we cannot achieve this on our own. We must believe that Jesus is God's Son, that He died for our sins, and that God raised Him from the dead so that we can have eternal life. Jesus is the only way to salvation, abundant life now, and life in heaven in the future.

Casting Notes: For a large group of clowns, play characters as listed. For a smaller group, one clown can play the three different parts of the Robber, the Staggering Clown, and the Toll Clown.

Prop Notes: Make the map by copying a road map onto one side of two sheets of 8½-by-14-inch paper. Then tape the two sheets together to form one large sheet (17-by-28). Print the words *Map to Salvation and Eternal Life* and draw several clouds or doves, etc., on the outside and fold in road map fashion. Make the money bag from any type of drawstring bag or even a paper sack and print a dollar sign on it. Create oversized money on a copier (see "Portrait Perils"). Use a plastic soft drink bottle inside the brown paper bag for the Staggering Clown as glass bottles can break and cause injury. Make directional and street signs from poster board and purchase traffic signs from an educational supply store or reproduce them on poster board as well. Laminate or coat all signs with clear adhesive covering. Print directional signs on both sides of the arrow so that either direction could be used. Display Signs either by holding them in hands or attaching them to posts.

Appendix B
An Initial Clowning Workshop for Youth

This appendix contains an outline for a four-hour basic clowning workshop designed for youth. Use the outline as a one-day event or present it in two or more shorter sessions. Require all clowning ministry members and leaders to attend the workshop, and repeat the same program annually for new clowning members.

The suggested outline has been effective in teaching basic clowning techniques; however, it is offered as a suggestion only. Add other ideas or topics as needed; adapt exercises and group activities to fit the size and interests of a particular ministry.

There are several handouts at the end of the workshop outline. These are available for duplication or you can alter them to meet specific ministry needs.

In order for the workshop to be most effective, secure an enthusiastic and energetic leader. Personal interest and excitement about the ministry are important; the leader will serve not only as an instructor but also as an encourager. A leader's own exaggerated, animated behavior and his or her laughter will make the difference between a workshop that imparts only information and one that not only teaches but excites and inspires youth as well.

Physical Setup

Ideally, conduct the workshop in a church fellowship hall or other large open area with both table space and ample floor space for movement. If you use such a facility, arrange for: (1) a learning area with table space for note taking during large-group lecture times; (2) a refreshment area with sufficient table space for serving and eating; (3) a clowning area with a large open area of floor space for practicing clowning techniques and skits; and (4) a makeup area with table space for both designing a clown face and for the actual application of makeup.

Decorations and Favors

Decorate the workshop area with brightly colored streamers, balloons, or posters to create a festive atmosphere. Arrange a table in the learning area with favors at each place (such as large clown sunglasses, silly hats, or even simple candy cups). Assemble copies of handouts to be used during the workshop, place them inside colored file folders, and set them at each seat along with different colored ink pens.

Supplies Needed

For general setup: Refreshments and paper products
Decorations
Favors
Copies of handouts
Ink pens
Camera, video camera, and film
Audiotape or compact disc player

For devotions: Bible
Balloons
Marker
Curling ribbon or string
Long balloon sticks
Brick covered with aluminum foil or large vase containing cube of floral foam

For technique exercises: Props for selected skits

For practice skits: Props for selected skits
Audiotapes or compact discs of background music

For worship as a part of clowning: Appropriate contemporary Christian music on audiotapes or compact discs

For one-on-one activities: Supplies appropriate for selected activities

For designing a clown face: Instruct youth to bring their complete makeup kits to the workshop. Have on hand extra paper towels, vegetable oil or cold cream, washcloths, applicators, etc.
Colored pencils

A CLOWNING WORKSHOP FOR YOUTH: LEARNING THE BASICS
(4-Hour Session)

I. WELCOME AND ANNOUNCEMENTS
(5 minutes; large-group activity)

Objective: To welcome new clowning ministry members and to explain the procedure for the workshop. Encourage and welcome questions or ideas at any time during the session.

II. DEVOTIONS AND OPENING PRAYER
(10 minutes; large-group activity)

Objective: To provide spiritual leadership and initiate a Christ-centered ministry.

Advance Preparation: Inflate 12 colorful balloons (with helium if possible). (Note: If helium is not available, attach balloons to long sticks.) Use a permanent marker and write one of the following words or phrases on each balloon: *Hungry, Something to Eat, Thirsty, Something to Drink, Stranger, Invited In, Needed Clothes, Clothes, Sick, Looked After, Prison, Visited.* Attach a length of colored curling ribbon to each balloon and tie (or set) one or two at each place in the learning area. (Note: For helium balloons that will be tied to the brick later, make ribbon length at least 2 to 3 feet. For balloons placed on sticks, ribbon is for decorative purposes only and you can cut it about 12 inches long and curl it.)

What to Do: Ask one youth to stand near the front of the room to receive balloons as they are brought forward. Read Matthew 25:35–40, pausing slightly between phrases. As the Bible verses are read, youth with the corresponding balloons will bring them to the front to form a large bunch. Once the balloons are collected, you can tie them to a brick covered with aluminum foil (if helium-filled) or place them in a large vase containing a block of floral foam (if on sticks). Add the bouquet of balloons to the refreshment table as decoration.

Use the following devotional thought to show how a clowning ministry can meet the needs of others and encourage youth in their concern for lost people.

Devotional Thought: Throughout Jesus' ministry on earth, He provided a standard by which all Christians are to model their own ministry to others in need. He stepped across social and racial boundaries; He loved the unlovable; He sought out and met physical needs. He taught people using examples from their personal lives and situations with which they were already familiar. In doing so, Jesus revealed God's love and mercy to a world desperately in need of spiritual healing.

Our world is still desperately in need of spiritual healing. As Christians, God has commissioned us to show that love and mercy to others. Clowning ministries step across social and racial boundaries; love the unlovable; and meet physical needs. The skits we can present will teach people by showing them situations with which they are already familiar. Using humor, laughter, and joy, we can follow Jesus' example.

Members of a clowning ministry show a concern for their world by making a commitment to serve God in such a unique way. They may not yet fully understand how or where they can meet needs; but with each kind action they offer, with each smile they give away, with each word of assurance they speak, with each laugh they encourage—God will reveal His love and mercy to the world. And the clowns will have touched "one of the least of these" and made an eternal difference in someone's life.

Lead in prayer.
- Give thanks for youth who are enthusiastic about serving God.
- Ask God to guide the ministry as it prepares for witnessing opportunities that lie ahead.
- Commit the ministry to serving God and give Him the glory for all you will accomplish.

III. INTRODUCTION TO CHRISTIAN CLOWNING
(10 minutes; large-group activity)

Objective: To outline expectations for participation in the clowning ministry and to provide a description of Christian clowning and how it differs from secular clowning.

What to Do: Begin by sharing any expectations you have for behavior and participation in the clowning ministry. This will establish boundaries and help to avert potential problems later.

Using the information in chapter 2, lead the ministry members to understand the basic concepts of Christian clowning and how Christian clowning differs from secular clowning.

Refer to handout 1, "What Is Christian Clowning?" and review the items listed.

IV. AN OVERVIEW OF THE BASICS
(10 minutes; large-group activity)

Objective: To explain the difference between good clowning and merely acting silly and to provide an overview of basic techniques for effective clowning.

What to Do: Explain that performance is not the goal of the clowning ministry but that it is still important to practice diligently and to be as professional as possible. This is not to win the praise of an audience but to enable the ministry to give its best to God and be able to hold an audience's attention until it conveys a message. In order to gain this professional image, it is necessary to learn and practice some basic techniques of clowning.

Explain that clowning is not a talent—it is a technique. And because it is a technique, anyone can learn it. Good clowning is *not* simply acting foolish or silly. The mark of a good clown is his or her ability to respond to circumstances in unexpected ways, not in silly ways. Clowns do not do funny things . . . they do ordinary things in funny ways. A person cannot *be* a clown . . . he or she must *become* a clown. Just as each person is a unique individual, each clown character has his or her own personality. It takes some time for this personality to blossom. Encourage youth to try a variety of clowning roles during this development process.

Outline the basic clowning techniques that you will explore during this workshop:

- showing emotions and attitude through facial expressions and by using the whole body

- exaggerating actions by making them larger than normal and doing them at a slower than normal speed

- connecting with an audience using direct eye contact

Refer to handout 2, "Helpful Hints for Good Clowning," and review the items listed.

V. LEARNING TO SHOW EMOTION
(20 minutes; small-group activity)

Objective: To explain the importance of showing emotion as a means of building a relationship with an audience and to have youth actively participate in exercises to learn this basic clowning technique. Youth will also learn to be more aware of their emotions and will become comfortable expressing them in an exaggerated way.

What to Do: Move to a large, open floor area and divide youth into smaller groups of four to six or less. Ask youth in each small group to stand in a circle facing one another, allowing sufficient room for large arm movement. Instruct members of each small group to wave to the other youth in their circle. As they begin waving, tell them to then double the size of their wave to give each other a real clown welcome.

Discuss with youth the importance of expressing emotions and attitudes in clowning. A good clown is constantly aware of his or her emotions and how quickly they change. Without the expression of emotion, an audience will not be able to empathize with the clown or his predicament. Emotions, attitudes, and feelings are those things that connect a clown to the audience. While emotion is primarily shown with facial expressions, the exaggerated use of arms and legs and other body movements will intensify the feeling and will draw an audience into the action.

Explain that clowns express emotions, attitudes, or feelings in an exaggerated fashion. They open their eyes wider than normal, smile broader than normal, and make body movements and gestures larger than normal. To practice facial expressions, ask small groups to wave at one another again; but you will now give them several different emotional clues that will determine *how* they are to wave. Emphasize that youth are to express any emotions they personally feel inside and not merely to imitate another person.

Read the following list of situations aloud, pausing slightly after each emotion to allow youth time to express it. (Emotions or attitudes to be expressed are shown in bold italics.)

- Wave to the others in your circle and let them know ***you are really excited to see them!***

- Imagine the person in front of you is waving frantically to you from a distance. You feel you should wave back to her or him, but *you are not really sure just who he or she is.*

- You want to say hello to the people in your circle, but *you are so shy that you can only manage a meek little wave.*

- Your neighbor has just spotted you at the movies when you told your parents you were at a church outing. Oh well, she's seen you now and even though *you're totally embarrassed* and sure that she'll tell your parents where you were, you have to wave back.

- A guy (or girl) you have had your eye on for quite some time has just walked in the door. You wave in a *flirtatious manner*.

- Now, think about what kind of basic personality you have and give the people in your circle one last wave that *expresses your own unique personality.*

Explain that the expression of individual emotions is an important clowning technique to master but that the ability to express constantly *changing* emotions is one trademark of a good clown. Sometimes emotions will change quickly; at other times, they will build and change more slowly. To be an effective clown, a person needs to be aware of appropriate emotions or attitudes and then express those feelings, not just with facial expressions but with the whole body. Provide several examples and demonstrate how the addition of arm and leg gestures or body movements can indicate the intensity of an emotion or attitude. (Add your own ideas to the examples given in chap. 4.)

Review the list of emotions suggested in chapter 4 and have all youth practice expressing them.

Suggest that youth continue to practice expressing exaggerated facial expressions at home in front of a mirror or to spend some time each day concentrating on the emotions they are feeling and to express those spontaneously with overstated facial expressions.

Instruct small groups to listen as you read a series of changing emotions. Instruct all youth to express these emotions in the most exaggerated way they can think of using as much of the whole body as possible. Youth should practice sustaining one expression of emotion until you indicate a change. (Read the following series aloud in a continuous fashion, pausing just long enough for youth to feel and express each emotion. Emotions to be expressed are shown in bold italics.)

- You are *happy*;
- so happy that you are feeling *a little giddy*.
- Now, you're still happy, but in a more *serene and contented* way.
- What's this?! You've just received some bad news and you are *very sad*.
- In fact, you are *sobbing uncontrollably*.
- At last, the tears are drying up. This certainly has been a long day and you are *feeling sleepy*;
- so sleepy that *you can hardly drag yourself to bed*.
- You finally make it to bed only to find that *it is freezing cold* in your bedroom!
- You become a *little irritated* as you notice an open window.
- Just as you reach out to close the window, a crack of thunder booms out *scaring you nearly to death* and you are forced to dive beneath the bedcovers!

Ask each small group to choose one person to participate in a short skit. Explain to the selected youth that you will read aloud a simple skit and that as they listen, they are to act out the scene expressing any emotions or attitudes they feel. Encourage youth to express emotions they are actually feeling inside and not just those they think might be correct.

Remind youth that the purpose of facial expression and body movement is to get an audience to feel the same emotions as the clown. To do this, they must use as much of their body as possible in the expression and should make direct eye contact with the audience. Some action takes place in the practice skit; however, the emphasis of this exercise is on expressing emotion. Let youth pantomime a practice skit one at a time. Use either the practice skit in chapter 4 ("Flying By") or "The New Kid at School" which follows.

THE NEW KID AT SCHOOL

Number of Clowns: One

Props: Chair
   Notebook or schoolbooks

A clown is walking down the hall at school one day and sees her (or his) best friend. Naturally, she is very excited and waves to get the friend's attention. The clown just can't wait to tell her friend all about another friend's cousin's sister who knows this guy whose name escapes her just now but who she still wants to go out with anyway.

Phew! Somebody just walked by that hasn't had a bath in several days . . . maybe even weeks! Who was that guy anyway?

Yikes! The bell just rang. Rats! That means it's time to go to class. As the clown turns to head for room 3B, she suddenly realizes . . . oh, no! My history book is nowhere to be found! Oh, man! Now, she remembers—it's still in the car. Oh, well. Mrs. Mortimer will understand.

After rushing against the traffic flow of scurrying students, the clown finally makes it into the classroom, sits down, and immediately starts whispering to her friends. Mrs. Mortimer comes in and slams her books down on the desk, scaring the clown half to death and certainly snapping her to attention. Boy, is Mrs. Mortimer ever mad! The clown slinks down into her seat to avoid being seen. She certainly doesn't want to have to tell about that missing history book now!

The bell rings out. Great! The clown has been saved by the bell and is quite relieved. Just then, a new student walks into the classroom and the clown gives him the once-over.

Hey. Wait a minute here. He looks vaguely familiar . . . hmmm. The clown sniffs the pungent air. What *is* that horrible odor? Yuck! Now, she remembers. The new kid is that guy she smelled in the hallway earlier and he's coming to sit in the desk right in front of her!

Could this day possibly get any worse? Just as the clown is contemplating the situation, Mrs. Mortimer calls out the name of the new student. No! It just can't be! Say it isn't true! It's the guy that the clown's friend's cousin's sister knows that she wanted to go out with! How humiliating! There's nothing left for the clown to do but put her head down on the desk in total shame and disbelief!

VI. ADDING MOTION TO EMOTION
(20 minutes; small-group activity)

Objective: To demonstrate the technique of pantomime movement as a means to clearly communicate action to an audience and to have youth actively participate in exercises to learn this basic clowning technique. Youth will become aware of action as a series of planned steps and will learn to make movements in an exaggerated style and at a slower than normal speed.

What to Do: Explain that clowning skits are basically a combination of emotion and motion, or action. Some action takes place, and the clown reacts to it with an emotion or with some type of movement. It is the manner in which a clown reacts to a situation that makes it humorous.

Youth should remember that all clowning action is planned action and consists of any number of individual steps to be completely communicated through pantomime. (Use the example of picking an apple from chap. 4 or one of your own to demonstrate how a simple action is broken down into a series of smaller movements.)

Explain that in addition to being executed step-by-step, all clowning action must be done slower than normal and exaggerated about twice as large as normal. The reason for this is so that an audience can clearly identify the action and so that they can see the action from a distance.

With youth back in small group circles and all youth participating, explain that you will read aloud some simple actions for them to pantomime. Remind youth to do each action slowly and in an exaggerated style as if they are trying to communicate the action to someone across the room. Inform youth that after they have a general feel for the basic action, they will then be given a particular situation that will require them to alter their expression and possibly the action itself to reflect the changing circumstances. Again, remind youth that they are all different people, and their clown characters will be different as well. Each youth should express what he or she is thinking and feeling, not just what others are doing around them. Encourage youth to use their own "clown within."

Read the following list of actions, pausing slightly after each to allow youth time to express them. Keep reminding youth to enlarge movements and slow down action.

- Dial a telephone (do not mention whether it is rotary or push button).
    Now, dial the telephone . . .
    - and realize you got a wrong number.
    - when it's a dire emergency and you are in a panic.
    - after you've just painted your fingernails.

- Open a door.
    Now, open the door . . .
    - when you are not quite sure what might be behind it.
    - when you are expecting a dream date.
    - when you are nervous about going into a classroom for a final exam.
    - when the door sticks and you have to pull so hard that the door ends up hitting you in the face. *(Be sure youth are reacting to the door hitting them by reeling backwards, expressing pain or irritation, etc.)*

- Comb your hair.
    Now, comb your hair . . .
    - when it's as long as you are tall.
    - when you've just come inside after being in a terrible wind storm.
    - when you're in a hurry to catch a ride.
    - when you have a cowlick that will absolutely *not* behave.

- Shake out a rug.
    Now, shake out the rug . . .
    - when it's much, much bigger than you are.
    - when you're facing into the wind.
    - when it's full of dust.

- Open a window.
    Now, open the window . . .
    - and after it's open you realize it's too windy outside.
    - when it's stuck and won't budge.
    - when it's really hot inside and you are dying for fresh air and you stick your head outside to breathe in the air . . . and the window slides down hitting you in the head.

If time permits, select a few of the practice examples in chapter 4 and ask all youth to exaggerate the suggested action.

Ask each small group to choose one youth to participate in a short practice skit. Explain that you will read aloud an ordinary scene and that they are to pantomime the action and to add expressions of any emotions or attitudes they are feeling. Remind youth that the audience needs to know not only what they are doing but how they feel about what is happening. Encourage them to make eye contact. (Note: If there is more than one small group, either have one youth in each group act out the skit simultaneously within the circles or have youth take turns in front of the entire group.) Read aloud the following skit, "Stuck Up," as the youth react. Do not read aloud the italicized actions unless youth are having difficulties with their own ideas.

STUCK UP

(In this skit, he, his, and him are intended to also refer to she, hers, and her.)

Number of clowns: One
Props: None

A very dignified clown enters casually walking down the street, minding his own business. *(The clown enters whistling, displaying somewhat of a smug attitude, possibly waving or tipping a hat to the audience.)* Suddenly, his foot gets stuck on something and he can't move it. *(The clown keeps walking along, acknowledging the audience but when he moves to take a step, one foot remains stuck to the floor. He looks at the audience while tugging a few more times with his leg. At last he turns to see what the problem is, grabs his leg, and begins pulling a little harder now. Still, the foot won't budge.)*

He takes a look at the situation from all sides. *(Still trying to maintain an air of dignity, the clown bends down to take a look at the front of the foot. Then he leans back to survey the heel. After checking the sides, he wiggles his fingers and reaches down, slowly and carefully pulling on the toe of his shoe.)* Yuck! It's chewing gum. *(The clown pantomimes the chewing of gum, pulling strands out from his mouth or blowing bubbles, etc., to indicate to the audience what the substance is.)* And those were his good shoes, too. Rats! *(The clown stomps his free foot on the ground in frustration.)*

Disgusting as it is, there is nothing to do but reach down and pull the gum off his shoe.

(The clown wiggles his fingers again and expresses distaste for the task before reaching slowly down to his shoe. He pries up the toe and the foot pops up and he scrapes the gum off the bottom of his shoe.) At last, the gum is off the shoe and the clown surely is glad. *(The clown stomps his foot on ground and pulls it up several times to show that the gum has been removed.)*

But wait! *(Sudden look of bewilderment, then a slow turn to look at the hand that scraped the gum off the shoe.)* Oh, no! Now the gum is stuck to the clown's fingers! *(Express sadness and indicate the predicament to the audience.)* The clown tries shaking the gum off his fingers. That doesn't work. How exasperating!

Aha! The clown has an idea! *(A sudden smile crosses the clown's face, his eyes open wider and he raises an index finger to indicate he has an idea .)* He tries using the other hand to pull the gum off his fingers and is delighted when he is successful *(Expresses delight and pride to the audience)*. But . . . uh-oh *(face changes again to bewilderment)*. The clown realizes that now the gum is stuck to his other hand!

Aha! Another idea! The clown places his hand carefully on the ground, pulling some of the gum out to the side. He then places his foot on the protruding piece of gum and with some amount of effort *(As clown tugs on the hand, the gum might cause it to snap back toward the floor before.)* he pulls his hand free from the gum. Ta-da! Now *both* hands are free of gum! *(Clown proudly displays both hands to audience.)*

The clown brushes his hands together smugly and starts to walk away, but his foot is stuck to the street once again. Oh, no! It cannot be! *(Clown makes eye contact with audience and as his face changes from prideful delight to disappointment, he slowly turns to look at the situation.)* But it is true. The clown's shoe is stuck just like it was to begin with.

The clown is really frustrated now. But he gets yet another idea! He reaches down, unties his shoe, and leaves it stuck to the gum as he walks away with a slight limp, but is just as dignified as when he entered.

VII. CONNECTING WITH AN AUDIENCE
(20 minutes; individual participation within large group)

Objective: To introduce the concept of drawing an audience into the action and to explain various types of clowning takes. Youth will have an opportunity to actively participate in exercises to learn this technique.

What to Do: Explain to youth that it is critical for an audience to feel like they are a part of all clowning action so that they remain interested until they receive the message. A clown needs to watch an audience just as the audience watches the clown. We accomplish this by using eye contact and what is termed *takes* in clowning.

Refer to handout 3, "Connecting with an Audience," and review the items listed. Demonstrate and have youth practice a variety of takes to create their own ideas.

Use the skit, "Dental Woes," from chapter 4 incorporating the suggested clowning takes. Review the basic storyline for the skit before beginning and repeat the skit several times so that several, if not all, of the youth are involved. Remind youth to incorporate all the clowning techniques they have been learning—expressing emotion, using exaggerated action, and connecting with an audience—as they pantomime the skit. Once the youth are familiar with the basic storyline, add background music to the action.

VIII. BREAK/REFRESHMENTS
(15 minutes)

IX. SIMPLE SKITS
(30 minutes; individual participation within large group)

Objective: To inform youth about the structure of skits and the types of skits that you will use in your clowning ministry and to provide practice time for them to use clowning techniques.

What to Do: Prior to the workshop, select skits for practice and gather appropriate props and background music. Select one or two of each type of skit—comic, inspirational, and message—from appendix A or other resources. Review the purpose and characteristics of each type of skit before asking youth to volunteer for character roles.

Refer to handout 4, "About Skits," and review the information listed. Then, practice simple skits. Repeat any skits that are of particular interest to the youth, changing volunteers each time. Remind youth to utilize the clowning techniques they have been learning and to rely on their "inner clown."

Before any action begins, explain the story line of the skit. Use background music as youth pantomime the actions. Encourage participating youth to interact with the audience (i.e., remaining youth and leaders) through direct eye contact and clowning takes. Reward each presentation by leading the audience in thunderous applause!

X. WORSHIP AS A PART OF CLOWNING
(20 minutes; large-group activity)

Objective: To introduce the concept of worship as a part of clowning and to determine how worship can be incorporated into clowning programs. Youth will be able to actively participate in a worship interpretation.

What to Do: Prior to the workshop, determine one particular type of worship that your ministry will use. Make plans to allow youth to actively participate in a demonstration of this activity.

Reiterate that the purpose of a Christian clowning ministry is to reveal Jesus Christ and show God's love. With this purpose in mind, conclude each clowning program with some type of worship.

Introduce one particular type of worship that the ministry will use. Lead youth to actively participate in a short demonstration. Select the worship portion of a clowning program to tie into the overall theme, leaving the audience with an inspirational or motivational message. The type of worship you choose will depend on personal preferences, interests, and talents. It may be one of the following.

- **Music Pantomime**. This form of worship uses a contemporary worship song with clowns actually pantomiming action to portray a scene that interprets the words of the song. If you choose this option, spend time explaining the use of pantomime interpretation and allow youth to participate in a demonstration. "Go Light Your World" and "Arise, My Love" are two good choices.
- **Sign Language.** This form of worship uses a contemporary worship song. Clowns use sign language to interpret the song. Training for this worship form should include a review of the basic sign language alphabet. Teach youth to fingerspell their names. Teach signs for a familiar hymn such as "Jesus Loves Me" with youth singing and signing the first verse for practice. Or teach signs to interpret the lyrics of a contemporary Christian song such as "His Eyes," "Follower," or "From This Moment On." Should you use a contemporary Christian song, do not expect to learn more than a verse or two in this first session. Ask youth to participate to become familiar with a few basic signs and with the process of interpreting lyrics using sign language.
- **Devotional Time.** Some ministries may simply end a clowning program by reading a Bible verse, expressing a devotional thought, or praying. Little actual training is necessary for this type of worship. However, a demonstration will allow youth to

understand how a devotional time will fit into the overall theme of a clowning program.

XI. ONE-ON-ONE ACTIVITIES
(20 minutes; large-group activity)

Objective: To introduce the concept of using one-on-one activities to create opportunities and to encourage youth in a conversational style of witnessing. Youth will also gain hands-on experience with at least one type of one-on-one activity.

What to Do: Prior to the workshop, determine at least one, or more if desired, one-on-one activity your ministry will use. Learn the techniques and have necessary supplies on hand.

Explain that one-on-one activities following clowning programs allow time for youth to interact with children and adults. The purpose of the activity is not purely for entertainment but rather to provide an activity that can result in the opportunity for a verbal witness.

Refer to handout 5, "Conversational Witnessing," and review the information presented.

Provide hands-on experience with the type(s) of one-on-one activity that your ministry will use. This will depend on personal preferences, interests, and abilities but might include one or more of the following

- **Face Painting.** Allow youth to practice face painting on each other. In particular have them try some conversational witnessing. Do face painting simply with water-based poster paints. Supply youth with small brushes, paper cups filled with clean water, and paper towels for blotting and cleanup.

  Encourage youth to paint patterns that can aid their witness. For example, a heart can remind someone of God's love; a flower can teach God's plan for creation; and so forth. Often, a child will ask for a specific design. Then the conversational witness will need to depend on the skills of the youth rather than on the design. Avoid using fictional characters or symbols of other non-Christian religions.
- **Balloon sculpturing.** This technique is easy to learn, intriguing to watch, and holds the attention of children as well as adults. Sculptures can include hats or simple animals. Resources for learning balloon sculpturing are available in local libraries or bookstores. It is best to use a balloon pump with these specialty balloons, as they are quite difficult to inflate. Demonstrate the basic twists and locking twists of balloon sculpturing. Then ask each youth to sculpt one or two different animals to take home.
- **Photographs or Prizes.** Make photographs with an instant picture camera or distribute small prizes following a clowning program. When children or adults come forward to receive prizes from a clown, you have an opportunity for conversation. While photographs and prizes do provide a means to spread a message in print and serve as a reminder of that message long after the clowning program is over, the length of one-on-one time is drastically reduced. Therefore, it is best to use photographs and prizes in conjunction with at least one other type of activity.

XII. BREAK/REFRESHMENTS
(15 minutes)

XIII. DESIGNING A CLOWN FACE
(45 minutes; individual activity within large group)

Objective: To provide guidance in designing of a unique clown face for each youth and to enable them to practice applying their own makeup.

What to Do: Prior to the workshop, give each youth a list of items they need for their makeup kits. Ask that each person bring his or her kit to the workshop. See chapter 5 for a list of needed items. Order the professional Clown White and color palates in bulk and give them out at the workshop, but ask youth to purchase all other items such as brushes, applicators, cold cream, powder, etc.

Refer to handout 6, "Clown Makeup," and discuss how a Christian clown's makeup is a reminder of his or her personal hope in Jesus Christ.

Explain that the exaggerated features of a clown's face help to expand facial expressions. Discuss the makeup style of the Auguste clown you will use during the workshop. (If you use a style other than Auguste, discuss your chosen style and adapt instructions on handouts.) Remind youth that the face they design may or may not be their permanent clown face. It may change as their clown character develops.

Refer again to handout 6, "Clown Makeup," and review the do's and don'ts of clown makeup.

Refer to handout 7, "Basic Makeup Designs," and review basic shapes for eyes, mouths, noses, eyebrows, and special features. Remind youth that these are the most basic designs and they are free to create their own. However, point out to them to make the face design simple and uncluttered. It is much easier to draw a design on paper than to apply that design to a face with makeup.

Allow youth time to design their own unique clown face on paper using the form on handout 8. Provide colored pencils that correspond to available makeup colors for youth to use.

As youth complete their design plans, ask them to move to a table where they can spread out their makeup supplies and let them re-create the design on their faces with makeup. Refer to handout 9, "Steps in Applying Makeup."

Be sure to take photographs of your emerging clowning ministry!

If time permits, let youth select skits they have learned during the workshop and perform them in full makeup. It will be surprising to see how much more like clowns they have become already!

XIV. CLOSING PRAYER

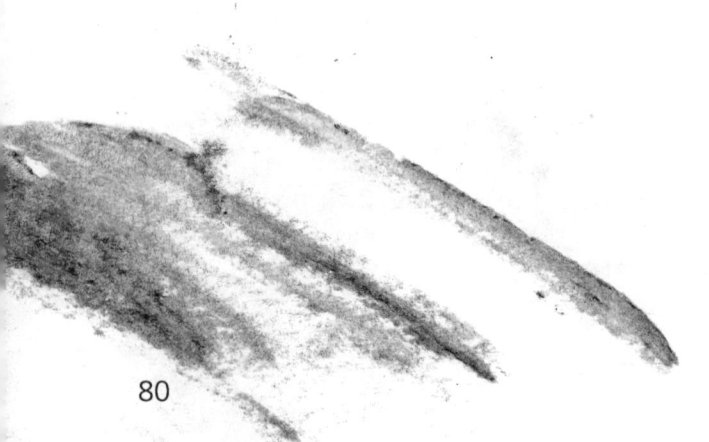

HANDOUT 1

WHAT IS CHRISTIAN CLOWNING?

"We are fools for Christ" (1 Cor. 4:10).

This partial Scripture verse does not mean that Christians should act foolishly or make fun of the gospel. By being a Christian and living our daily lives based on Christian values, our ways and actions seem "foolish" to non-Christians. We must help them understand by introducing them to Jesus Christ.

ABOUT CHRISTIAN CLOWNS*

Because clowns are a universally accepted symbol of joy and laughter, clowning has become a popular ministry that can share the gospel of Jesus Christ in areas where more traditional methods of witnessing are not effective. Christian clowns use ridiculous means to make the world aware of its predicament and then to present Christ as the solution. Here are a few things to remember about Christian clowning:

1. Clowns are universal and as such can communicate both good and evil. Christian clowns must keep Christ at the center of their ministry so that what they communicate is a revelation of God's love.

2. Because clowns are characters of fantasy, Christian clowns must not extend an invitation to children to make a decision for Christ. Any such decisions are based on a clear understanding of salvation and not because a beautiful clown encouraged it.

3. If a Christian clown leads in prayer (especially with children), he or she should first remove a wig, hat, plastic nose, etc., to indicate that he or she is now out of the fantasy and has entered reality for the prayer.

4. A Christian clown ministry should always have at least one member who is not in costume. This always leaves someone available for prayer or to talk with children about decisions.

5. A Christian clown character is *not* real and cannot have a salvation experience. A clown *can*, however, give his or her own personal testimony but should be certain the person knows the difference between the clown as a real person and the character he or she has portrayed.

*Adapted from comments by Everett Robertson in *The Ministry of Clowning*.

HELPFUL HINTS FOR GOOD CLOWNING

Good clowning is a technique, not a talent. Anyone has the capability of becoming a clown, but it requires commitment and practice. Some basic tips to remember that will help develop your clown character and enhance your clowning technique are:

1. Show your emotions! The audience must know how you feel through *each* action. Show them how you feel by the way you execute the action. Every action should have some type of accompanying emotion, attitude, or feeling.

2. Express each action and emotion with your whole body. This requires concentration and practice. Use every possible part of your body.

3. Exaggerate all movements.

4. Do movements (actions) more slowly than normal. This will help the audience follow the action. The greater the distance between the clown and the audience, the slower the movements.

5. Focus on one action at a time. Concentrate on each action, keep it as simple as possible, and make it as sharp and clean as possible. Complete one action and be sure the audience understands it before going on to the next.

6. Move your lips to indicate speech during a silent skit.

7. When holding an imaginary object, be sure to leave space between the fingers as if the object were actually in your hand.

8. Always lead with your eyes! Let your eyes tell the audience where the action is going. Always keep our eyes on either the audience or the action.

9. *Never* turn your back to the audience. Occasionally, you may need to do this, such as when changing positions on the stage. However, be certain that all action and all emotions are in plain view of the entire audience.

10. Keep skits short and simple. Once you make a point, move on. Remember, it is the action and not the clowns themselves that are the point of a skit. Clowns should draw attention to the problem at hand, not to themselves.

HANDOUT 3

Connecting with an Audience

To keep an audience attentive and interested in a clowning program until you give the message, build a relationship so that they feel a part of the action. The best way to keep an audience's attention is with direct, deliberate eye contact and through what is known as the *clowning take*.

A clowning take is an action done at any time during a skit or routine that occurs when a clown momentarily takes his attention off the other clowns and activity to make direct eye contact with a member or section of the audience. During this connection, the clown relates an emotion or thought, imparts information, shares a laugh, gives a direction, indicates a secret, or asks a question.

TYPES OF CLOWNING TAKES

Greeting Take: Occurs during the entrance of a skit and greets or acknowledges the audience, sets the mood, and gives a feeling of place or setting.

Information Take: Indicates to the audience some logical action that is about to take place before it actually happens.

Devious Take: Indicates to the audience that the clown is about to do something sneaky or underhanded before that action actually happens.

Secrecy Take: Usually involves touching a finger to the lips to keep the audience quiet, then lets them in on a secret about what is going to happen, where something is hidden, or who is responsible for a certain mistake.

Opinion Take: Involves the audience in a decision the clown is about to make.

Attitude, or Feeling, Take: Occurs when a clown shares a greater intensity of emotion or mocks another clown (*never* an audience member!).

Idea Take: Occurs any time a clown has a brilliant idea.

HANDOUT 4

About Skits

The Structure of Skits

Generally, all clowning skits follow a simple format.

Entrance (or Opening): The clown greets the audience and sets the place, mood, and sometimes the situation.

The Exposition: The audience becomes aware of the situation or understands it more clearly.

The Conflict: Some type of conflict between clowns or between a clown and an object occurs.

The Solution: This occurs only after a few ridiculous failures, and is either successful or results in an unexpected disaster.

The Exit: The clowns complete the action and leave the audience with the desired thought or emotion.

Types of Skits Used in a Clowning Ministry

1. **Comic skits** are designed strictly for entertainment and attracting attention. They are used by a clowning ministry to build a relationship with an audience.

2. **Inspirational skits** depict some type of moral value. They usually involve a decision between right and wrong and a clown must resolve a problem in a manner consistent with biblical values. The concluding thought teaches a lesson to the audience.

3. **Message skits** reveal specific biblical truths. Clowns are involved in situations in which behaviors need to be changed. At some point during the skit, a clown realizes the sinfulness of his situation and turns to God. The biblical truth is revealed and the concluding thought causes the audience to contemplate their own spiritual condition.

HANDOUT 5

CONVERSATIONAL WITNESSING

Conversational witnessing speaks more through actions than words. In clowning situations, time with children, youth, and even adults will be greatly limited—often only a few minutes. During this time the clown must establish a relationship, put the person at ease, and offer a simple witness.

Use activities such as face painting, balloon sculpturing, or prizes following a clowning program to provide opportunities for this one-on-one time. As a face is being painted or as an animal is sculpted from a balloon, a conversation can easily take place.

Tips for Conversational Witnessing

1. Always focus on the *person*, not the clown.
   a) Tell the person how glad you are that he or she attended.
   b) Ask where the person is from, where he or she attends school, etc.
   c) Find something positive to say or compliment about the person.

2. Draw attention to the clowning program's message. Ask which skit the person enjoyed the most. If it is a message skit, discuss the message of that skit in your conversation. If a message skit is not chosen, tell what you liked about the chosen skit and then add why you also like a particular message skit and retell that message in your conversation. (Example: "One of my favorite skits was [*name of message skit*]. It makes me feel good to know God loves us so much that He sent Jesus to be our Savior.")

3. Always make your last comment a positive one.

What to Do in Difficult Situations

There may be times when it will be difficult to give any kind of conversational witness. An obstinate child or a rude young person may wish to have his or her face painted or to receive a balloon but may be antagonistic in the process. If you can comfortably work a witnessing statement into a conversation, do so. If not, the witness will simply be love in action—still a powerful tool in God's hand!

Clown Makeup

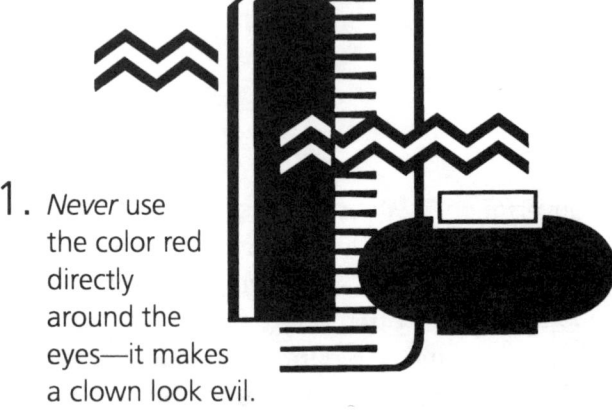

Makeup is an important element of clowning. The face expresses the style of the clown, his emotion, character, and life. The exaggerated features of the makeup let the audience know they are about to see life expanded and enlarged.

The process of putting on the face is a ritual for the clown. It is the moment he escapes from a world of pain and fear into the fantasy of the innocent clown in a perfect world. For a Christian clown, makeup is a reminder of the saving grace of Jesus Christ. The white makeup is a symbol of Jesus' death. The colorful markings are symbols of life and represent the rebirth a Christian experiences when he or she accepts Jesus Christ. The old character dies and a new character is brought to life.

Designing Your Unique Clown Face

Make each clown's face different. Make a drawing of your clown face before trying it with makeup. This will allow you to try different combinations and determine if you have too many markings, too much of one color, features that are too large, etc. When planning your clown face, remember the following tips.

1. *Never* use the color red directly around the eyes—it makes a clown look evil.

2. *Never* use the colors green or blue around the mouth—they make a clown look sick.

3. Do not extend the edges of your clown mouth past the outside edges of your human eyes.

4. Keep your face design simple. The more markings you use, the more broken up your face will appear. Too many markings detract from emotions the clown shows.

5. Be sure to include a Christian symbol somewhere in your makeup, such as the Christian fish symbol on the face or the back of a hand, or a red dot on the nose or on the face.

HANDOUT 7

BASIC MAKEUP DESIGNS

EYES

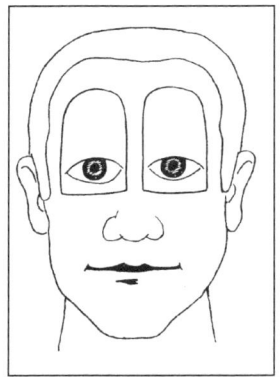
Tall Rounded

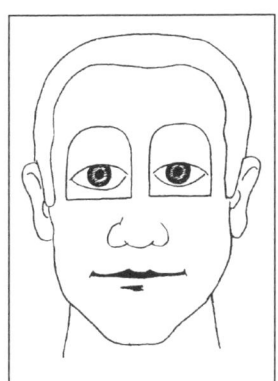
Short Rounded

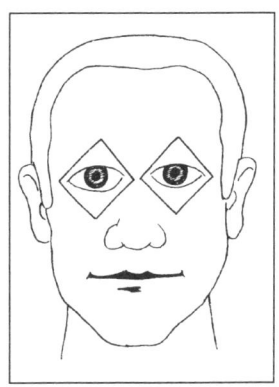
Diamond

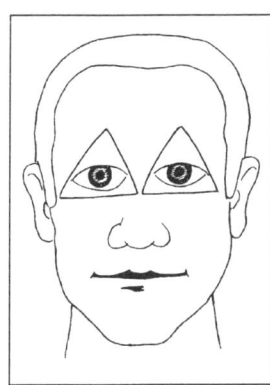
Triangle

MOUTHS

Basic Smile

Basic Smile with Attached Cheeks

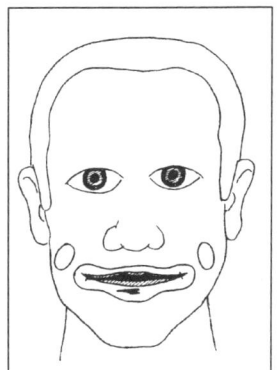
Basic Smile with Detached Cheeks

Basic Smile with Dropped Lower Lip

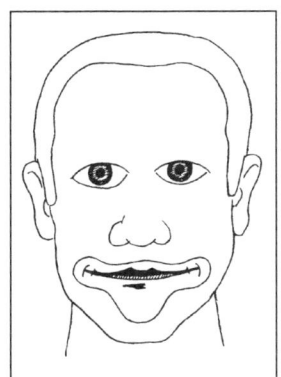
Thin Smile with Dropped Lower Lip

Baby-doll Lips

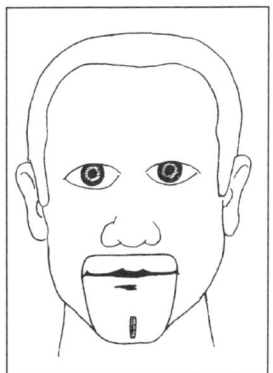
Hobo Mouth

87

NOSES (optional):

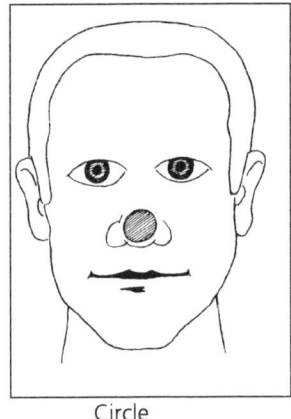
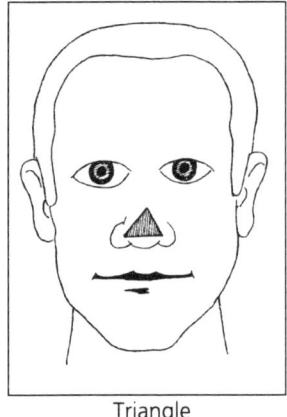

Circle　　　　　　　　Triangle　　　　　　　Inverted Triangle

EYEBROWS (used over short rounded eyes or on white makeup of tall rounded eyes):

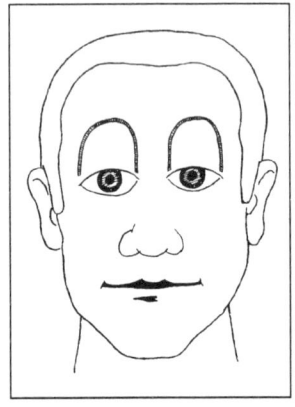
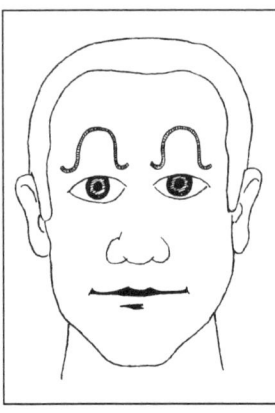
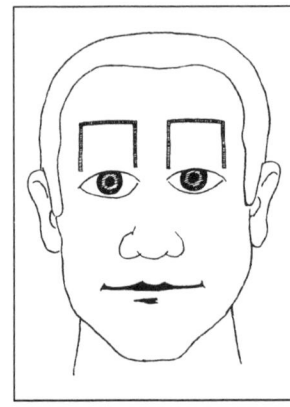
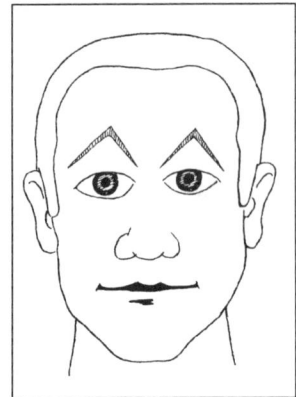

Rounded　　　　　　Curlycues　　　　　　Squared　　　　　　Tented

EYE ACCENTS (usually used in lieu of eyebrows):

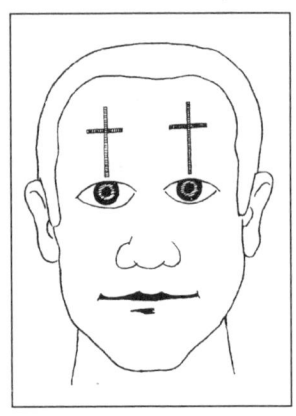
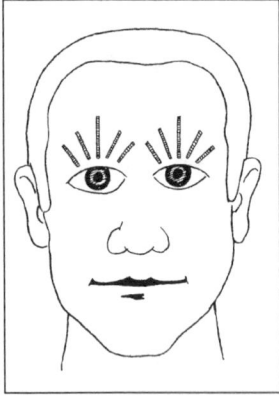
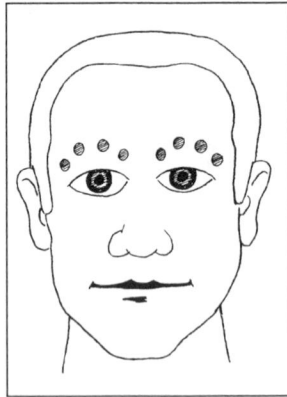
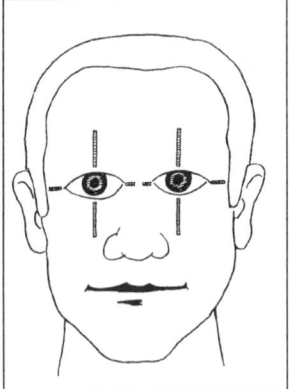

Cross Pattern　　　　Fan Pattern　　　　Arched Dots　　　　Single Line

EXTRA FEATURES

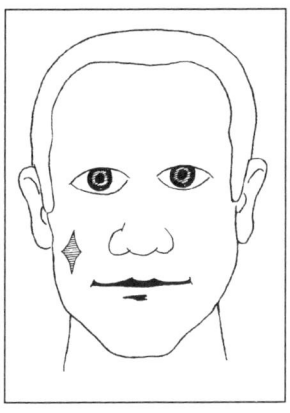
Diamonds

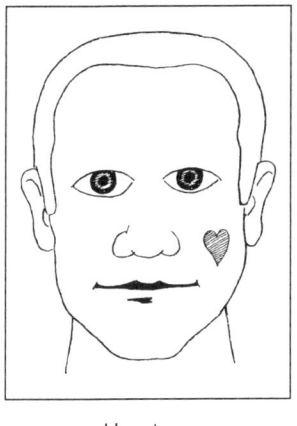
Hearts

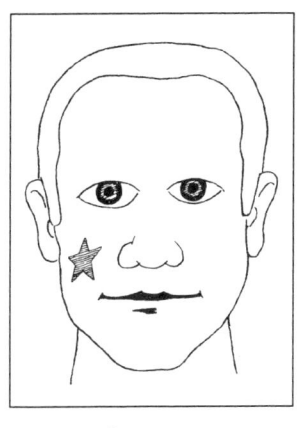
Stars

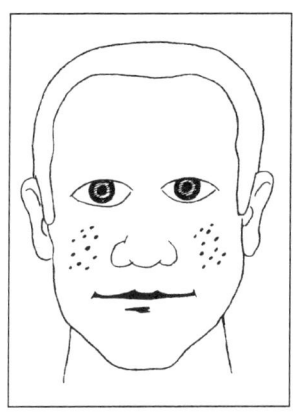
Freckles

Since the purpose of the ministry is to reveal Jesus Christ, use some type of Christian symbol as part of each clown's makeup. For example, use the Christian fish symbol either on the face or on the back of one hand, or a red dot on the nose or face.

SAMPLE FACES

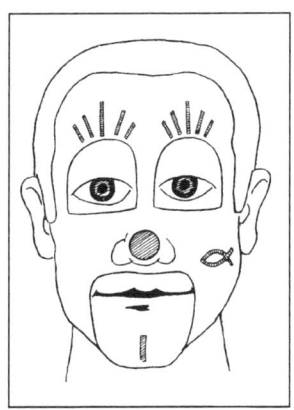
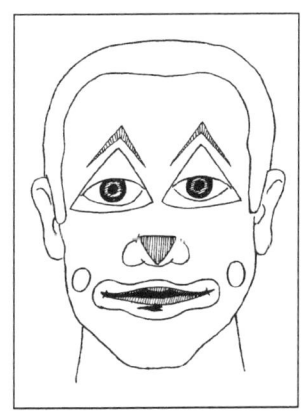
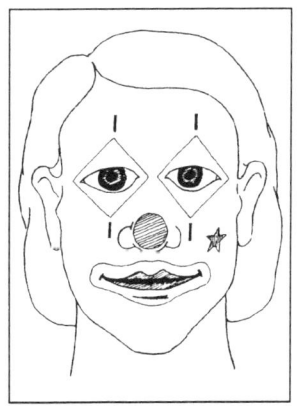

HANDOUT 8

HANDOUT 9

STEPS IN APPLYING MAKEUP

(A Basic Auguste-Style Face)

1. Apply a base coat of cold cream. Rub evenly all over your face. Pat off any excess with a paper towel.

2. Using an eyeliner pencil, draw in outlines for eyes and mouth.

3. Apply Clown White with fingertips or an applicator to the eye and mouth areas.

4. Lightly pat over the white areas with fingertips to create a smooth appearance.

5. Use a white sock containing baby powder and generously pat the powder on all white areas. *You cannot use too much powder!* This is what helps to set your makeup and keeps it from running, bubbling, or smearing.

6. Remove excess powder from skin areas with a soft-bristled brush. Brush lightly until all excess powder is removed.

7. Set makeup by spraying with a fine water mist.

8. Carefully add in colored markings to eyes, mouth, and nose (if desired).

9. Lightly powder the colored portions with a *separate* sock with baby powder. Be careful to touch only the colored areas.

10. Set the makeup with another fine water mist spray.

11. Redraw any black outlines if necessary.

12. Add a Christian symbol with an eyeliner pencil to either the face or back of a hand.

13. Remove makeup with vegetable oil or cold cream and tissue. *Do not scrub!* Then wash your face with mild soap and warm water.

14. To clean makeup brushes and applicators, dip them in vegetable oil and blot on a paper towel. Then soak in warm water and a mild soap. Pat dry.

RESOURCES AND BIBLIOGRAPHY

RESOURCES

Sources for Information About Clowning in General or Clowning as a Ministry
Check your local library or bookstore for these titles. Also read the bibliographies in each for additional resources.

Litherland, Janet. *The Clown Ministry Handbook*. Colorado Springs: Meriwether Ltd., 1989.

Meyer, Charles R. *How to Be a Clown*. New York: David McKay Company, 1977.

Robertson, Everett, comp. *The Ministry of Clowning*. Nashville: Broadman Press, 1983.

Sanders, Toby. *How to Be a Complete Clown*. New York: Stein and Day, 1978.

Shaffer, Floyd T. *If I Were a Clown*. Minneapolis: Augsburg Publishing House, 1984.

———. *An Introduction to Clown Ministry*. Colorado Springs: Meriwether Publishing Ltd., n.d. Filmstrip.

Stolzenberg, Mark. *Clown for Circus and Stage*. New York: Sterling Publishing Company, 1981.

Toomey, Susan Kelly. *Mime Ministry*. Colorado Springs: Meriwether Publishing Ltd., 1986.

Wiley, Jack. *Basic Circus Skills*. Harrisburg, PA: Stackpole Books, 1974.

Skit Sources
Contact Contemporary Drama Service, Box 7710, Colorado Springs, CO 80933, to request their mail order catalog of clown, mime, puppet, dance, and storytelling resources. They have a large number of skit booklets and clowning books available, including the following.

The Christian Clown by Ruth Hansen (6 skits).

The Clown as Minister I by Janet Litherland (7 skits).

The Clown as Minister II by Janet Litherland (5 skits).

Clown Hits and Skits by Richard Strelak and Marty Sherman (20 secular skits).

Clown Mimes for Christian Ministry I and *II* by Susie Kelly Toomey (9 and 8 skits, respectively).

The Clown's Balloons and Other Mime Sketches by Daniel Robb and Michael Sturko (5 secular skits).

Here Come the Clowns by Clarice Moon (secular content).

Contact Dewey's Good News Balloons, 1202 Wildwood Drive, Deer Park, TX 77536, for information on the following titles (all by Ralph Dewey).

Dewey's Gospel Clown Skits 1

Dewey's Clown Gags and Giggles

Dewey's Klown Komedy

Check your local library or bookstore for the following skit resources.

Feder, Happy Jack. *Clown Skits for Everyone.* Colorado Springs: Meriwether Publishing Ltd., 1991.

———. *Mime Time.* Colorado Springs; Meriwether Publishing Ltd., 1991.

Flosso, Jackie. *World's Best Clown Gags.* Compiled by Clettus Musson. Brooklyn: D. Robbins and Company, Inc., 1987.

Lamb, Buddy, comp. *Clown Scripts for Churches.* Nashville: Convention Press, 1991.

Litherland, Janet. *Everything New and Who's Who in Clown Ministry.* Colorado Springs: Meriwether Publishing Ltd., 1993.

McVicar, Wes. *Clown Act Omnibus.* Colorado Springs: Meriwether Publishing Ltd., 1987.

Sources for Props, Makeup, Balloons, Balloon Pumps, Prizes, and Other Clowning Supplies

Write and request mail order catalogs from the following companies.

Morris Costumes
4300 Monroe Road
Charlotte, NC 28205
(704) 333-4653

Oriental Trading Company
P. O. Box 2308
Omaha, NE 68103-2308
1-800-228-2269

Funhouse Magic Shop
3535 Belair Road
Baltimore, MD 21213

Mitzie's Clown Costumes and Gimmicks
1408 Main Street
Hopkins, MN 55343

Under the Big Top
3960-R Prospect Avenue
Yorba Linda, CA 92686

Sources of Information on Balloon Sculpturing

Hsu-Flanders, Aaron. *Balloon Animals.* Chicago: Contemporary Books, 1988.

Myers, T. *Designer Collection.* Self-published and available through Morris Costumes, 4300 Monroe Road, Charlotte, NC 28205.

Contact Dewey's Good News Balloons, 1202 Wildwood Drive, Deer Park, TX 77536, for information on the following titles (all by Ralph Dewey).

Dewey's Basic Balloon Sculpturing Course

Dewey's Extra Easy Balloons

Dewey's New Balloon Animals

Dewey's Gospel Balloon Routines #1, #2, and *#3*

Sources of Information on Sign Language

Lawrence, Edgar D. *Sign Language Made Simple*. Springfield, MO: Gospel Publishing House, 1975.

Reikehof, Lottie L. *The Joy of Signing*. Springfield, MO: Gospel Publishing House, 1978.

———. *Talk to the Deaf*. Springfield, MO: Gospel Publishing House, 1963.

BIBLIOGRAPHY

Bishop, George. *The World of Clowns*. Los Angeles: Brooke House Publishers, 1976.

Boyd, Rev. David. *Magic, Message and Humor for the Gospel Clown*. Self-published and available through Morris Costumes, 4300 Monroe Road, Charlotte, NC 28205.

Lamb, Buddy, comp. *Clown Scripts for Churches*. Nashville: Convention Press, 1991.

Litherland, Janet. *The Clown Ministry Handbook*. Colorado Springs: Meriwether Ltd., 1989.

———. *Everything New and Who's Who in Clown Ministry*. Colorado Springs: Meriwether Publishing Ltd., 1993.

McVicar, Wes. *Clown Act Omnibus*. Colorado Springs: Meriwether Publishing, Ltd., 1987.

Robertson, Everett, comp. *The Ministry of Clowning*. Nashville: Broadman Press, 1983.

Stolzenberg, Mark. *Clown for Circus and Stage*. New York: Sterling Publishing Company, 1981.

Toomey, Susie Kelly. *Mime Ministry*. Colorado Springs: Meriwether Publishing Ltd., 1986.

About the writer

Janice Petrea has served as an Acteens and youth leader for over 19 years, devoting much of that time training and leading youth to witness and minister. Following an Acteens Activators missions trip experience in 1993 (during which clowning played an integral part), she organized and continues to direct Whimsy & Worship, the clowning and signing ministry at Faith Baptist Church, Faith, North Carolina. She lives in Granite Quarry, North Carolina, with her husband, Troy, and their three daughters, Ginny, Erin, and Carrie, who are all involved in clowning. She holds a bachelor's degree from the University of North Carolina at Greensboro and is employed as executive vice-president of Institutional Development Associates.